Praise for *Turn Off the TV and . . .*

"I wish every parent, every child in America could have this source of inspiration." *—Robert Coles*

"Anne Rogovin's wonderful book teaches us how to recover the true magic of an active childhood."
—Stephen Jay Gould

"A sensitive and helpful book." *—Lowell P. Weicker, Jr.*

"The key to the future is learning to do things ourselves again. Science, technology, and modern electronic communication are all wonderful. But it's life that is miraculous. This book is a poem to life." *—Pete Seeger*

"There is a world of joy and excitement out there, one which makes television pale by comparison. Anne Rogovin's book gives this realization to all members of the family."
—Edward Asner

"An educational *tour de force* of elegant simplicity."
—Ralph Nader

"Turn the TV off and go outside. Move toward something green and growing, and as you walk, listen to your self."
—Ossie Davis

"Anne Rogovin has provided an unusually eas
us to infect our lives with critical doses of joy, w
love." *—Samuel J. Alessi, Jr.*

TURN OFF THE TV *and...*

ANNE ROGOVIN

Abingdon Press
Nashville

TURN OFF THE TV AND . . .

This book is printed on acid-free recycled paper.

Library of Congress Cataloging-in-Publication Data

Rogovin, Anne.
Turn off the TV and— / Anne Rogovin.
p. cm.
ISBN 0-687-00233-8 (acid-free paper)
1. Amusements. 2. Active learning. 3. Family recreation.
I. Title.
GV1201.R57 1995
790.1'91—dc20
94-44345
CIP

This book is dedicated to

My parents, whose lives taught me a little about "caring."

Milton, my husband, best friend, an idealist and photographer of the poor, the "forgotten ones."

Our children:

Ellen—an inner-city teacher in Philadelphia for thirty years

Paula—a teacher in New York City for twenty-one years and chairperson for Teachers Against Apartheid and Racism

Mark—muralist and founder of the Peace Museum in Chicago

Our grandchildren: David Steven Eric
Malaika Aliya

and

All the children of the world including the children in South Africa who have gained their freedom—at last! May all of them dream and work toward the fulfillment of their dreams.

95 96 97 98 99 00 01 02 03 04—10 9 8 7 6 5 4 3 2 1

MANUFACTURED IN THE UNITED STATES OF AMERICA

Special Thanks to:

Dr. Steven Piver—Chief of Gynecologic Oncology at Roswell Park Cancer Institute, President of the Board of Night People, and treasured friend, who saw my ignorance of computers and arranged to have my manuscript typed onto one for Abingdon Press.

Cheryl Blake—who worked so conscientiously for days and days retyping my manuscript onto a computer, doing a finer job than I could ever have done.

My whole family—who went over my manuscript from time to time and were the severest, sometimes the most painful critics anyone could have.

A special, special thanks to

Paula—for suggesting my title.
Eric—who pitched in with some great alternatives to television watching.
Aliya and Malaika—whose poetry is so beautiful, I had to include some for my readers to enjoy.
Alexander Anzelon, the wholesome young son of our friends Margaret Sullivan and Bud Anzelon who contributed some good, fun ideas too.

And to

Charles Kuralt
Robert Coles
Ralph Nader
Ed Asner
Stephen Jay Gould
Pete Seeger
Ossie Davis

all uncommon humanists, giving all their talents to the most beautiful thing in the world—the betterment of humankind

and yet

generously taking time to read my manuscript and give their thoughts about it.

"I love you,"
said a great mother.
"I love you for what you are
knowing so well what you are.
And I love you more yet, child,
deeper yet than ever, child,
for what you are going to be,
knowing so well you are going far,
knowing your great works are ahead,
ahead and beyond,
yonder and far over yet."

—Carl Sandburg, from *The People, Yes*

If I Could

If I could I would give you the flower
that brightens your day.
I would give you the rain that waters the earth,
and the trees that shade the forest.

If I could I would give you the moon that
shines at night. I would give you the stars that
fill the sky, and the sun that shines so bright.

If I could I would give you the birds'
songs that wake you up each morning. I would
give you the shells from the sea, and the
sand from the beach.

If I could.

—Aliya Hart
(for her mother, Ellen)

Foreword

It may seem odd for a man who makes his living in television to praise a book that advises turning the TV off. Let me explain:

My father was a lifelong social worker down home in North Carolina. He spent much of his life thinking about the needs of little children. In the 1940s, long before Head Start was conceived, he helped establish day-care centers in our county for the children of poor working mothers. He sold the idea to the County Commissioners as a way to keep the mothers off welfare, but his real interest was the children; he wanted to give them a daytime environment that would stimulate their curiosity about the world. My father had the notion, still has it, that by the age of six, a child's life already is pretty well formed, for good or ill. He or she will already have been well loved, or not, and will have known some successes and gained some confidence, and formed some interests and some childish ambitions, or not.

How I wish that Anne Rogovin's marvelous book, *Turn Off the TV and . . .*, had been available to the teachers in those early child development centers! Of course, there was not yet such a thing as TV to turn off, but the principle has been the same in all the ages of humanity: the lucky child is the one whose parents and teachers are able to give him a hunger for learning.

I was such a lucky child. What my father preached at work, he and my mother practiced at home. So I learned the joy of reading and rhyming and writing stories and dreaming dreams. On walks in the woods, I learned the names of all the plants and flowers. During household projects, I learned how bricks are laid and bookshelves are made and pictures are framed and bread is baked and strawberries are planted. Looking back, I see that I was a little boy of no money but much privilege. Nothing I absorbed sitting at a desk in school has served me half so well in life as the loving and never-to-be-forgotten gifts, the life-enhancing ones, the ones my parents gave me.

Anne Rogovin, who is a loving person, knows all this in her bones. So here is her gift, life-enhancing, to all parents and teachers, and to all children.

—Charles Kuralt

Some summer day—
Take off your shoes and socks
and
Walk barefoot in the cool, wet grass
(Doesn't it feel good to have the
earth under
your feet?)
Run barefoot in puddles
Stamp your feet on warm, wiggly mud
and
Let the mud squeeze in between your toes.
(Mud shouldn't make mothers mad because mud washes off easily in a pail or with the hose.)

Play "bakery" and sell the best pies in the whole world, the ones you make with the finest mud.

Wouldn't you love to do any of these things more than anything else in the world?

If it's nighttime—
Look outdoors.
Did everyone's light go on?
Did the birds stop singing?
Is the car parked in the garage?
Where did the squirrels go? Are they hiding up in the trees?
Are the bees in their hives and there's no more buzzing for the day?
Is your pussycat tired and has she stopped purring till tomorrow?
Are you tired too? Are you going to bed?

Get permission to walk in your father's shoes.
Don't they look like GIANT SHOES?

If your dad has an old pair, you could be a giant anytime!

 Enjoy a walk on a bright, sunny winter's day.

 Find a big clump of bushes
or
a patch of tall weeds
(they can be your jungle).
Sit in the middle of it.
Then just listen.
Sh Sh Sh.

Play with the empty carton that the new refrigerator came in.
The carton could be a regular everyday car—
or
would you like it to be a racing car?
(Never mind if you don't have wheels for the car. Your car doesn't have to have wheels.)
Your empty carton could also be:
a boat on the lawn
an animal's den
a hide-away house
a bed
an ocean liner
a spaceship
—a place to store your toys.
If you have more than one carton, they could be:
a fleet of buses, trains, or cars
lots of skyscrapers
houses on your block
a shopping plaza
or—
even a whole city.

Build a ship from chairs and be sure to have soft pillows to sit on.
Then go sailing away!

Play "lion and bear" with your friend.
You be the lion
and
let your friend be the bear.
The table could be your den.
You have to roar
and
roar
and
roar
and
your friend must growl
and
growl
and
growl.
And then—roar and growl some more!

Watch a bird.
Doesn't it seem to go wherever it wants to?
in the forest?
in the fields?
in the garden?
on a roof?
And it never needs to ask for permission either!
(Wouldn't it be nice to be a bird?)

Clean up the awful mess in your room.

Go sledding down the hill in the park.
If you don't have a sled, you can use an old tray for a sled.

On a soft summer night, when your grandparents are visiting, watch them dance together without music. They just hum.

Get out the old blankets and let them be tumbling mats.

Make some great big fat snowballs and bring them in the house to sit overnight.
Go get them in the morning.
LOOK—There's a big *puddle* on the floor!
Did you learn a lesson?
Now try this:
Next time put your snowballs in a freezer bag.
Put the bag in the freezer
and
Save them for the summertime—
or
a rainy day when you have nothing special to do.

Go outdoors and look around for a tree that has a hole in it. If you're lucky the hole may be an owl's nest!
Did you know that an owl's life is very different from most other birds'? Here's why:
An owl flies about at *night*—not like most other birds, which fly about by *day*.
While the owl flies about, he catches his food (mice—yes!).
And then he flies back to his nest and sleeps all *day!*
(No wonder children hardly ever see owls!) When we sleep, the owl is up, and when the owl is up, we sleep!)
Someday you may be lucky enough to hear an owl's call—and it will sound just like he's calling you.
YOU! YOU! YOU!

Put on your skates and zoom down to the corner store to buy some bread for Dad's lunch.

(When you skate to the store, it isn't like a job you have to do. Isn't it more like playing than working when you can skate?)

Have a grown-up make a bowl of sudsy water.
Get out your bubble-pipe
and
blow bubbles.

Enjoy a day with the family at a seashore.
Think of all the things you can do! You can:

Look for ships coming and going.
Listen to the sound of the sea.
(Doesn't it seem to go on forever?)
Do you hear the cry of a seagull?
Walk along the shore and look for shells.
(How many different shells can you find after a night's rainstorm?)
(Do you hear the sea in one of the seashells?)
Are you lucky enough to see a bird catching a fish?
Is there a crab that got washed up on the beach?
Watch the waves come curling down the beach, pushing the sand into pretty ripples.
Dig wells in the sand.
Look for a piece of driftwood you can bring home with you to use as a centerpiece for the dining room table.
If you wet the sand, you can make pies and cakes for a bakery.
Do you think you'd like to picnic in the sand?
Build a castle so big anyone would be able to walk in it.
Then watch the castle disappear as the tide washes in.
And then, make another one.

Collect all the shoe boxes
egg cartons
and

empty jars
about the house and from your neighbors.
They're great for storing:
crayons
pencils
felt-tip markers
chalk
paper dolls
and other valuable things.

Search for a caterpillar in your backyard.
If you're lucky enough to find one—pick it up and let it crawl up your hand.
(Did it tickle?)

Watch the caterpillar as it goes along.
(Isn't it pretty smart to crawl over the stone that's in its way?)

Why not be a caterpillar too?
Get on your belly and
slowly, slowly, slowly
inch by inch by inch
crawl along.
(Did you get very far? You didn't—did you? Well—now you know a little of what it feels like to be a caterpillar. They just never ever seem to be in a hurry!)

Hold onto your mother's hand
and
walk on the low brick wall of the nearby building.
(After all—isn't this what walls are for?)

(If it's wintertime) look at the stiff branches and jagged twigs of the trees.

Isn't it hard to think that these same stiff branches and jagged twigs will turn green and bloom in the spring and bear fruit?

Watch your fat cat snoozing on the porch.

ZZZZZZZZZZZZZZZZ

Do you think she's dreaming of a mouse?

Be very quiet for just five minutes.

Sh Sh Sh!

What were you thinking?

Play store with:

some real fruits and vegetables like: potatoes, apples, oranges, etc.
some unopened canned goods
buttons for money
an empty egg carton as a cash register
a pad and pencil for taking orders
and
a doll carriage or wagon for a shopping cart.

And now you're ready for business.

Visit the empty lot nearby just to see if anything lives there.

Oh—yes!

See—there are squirrels
rabbits
a chipmunk
wildflowers (and one is waiting just for you!)
birds (the bird isn't there while you're there—but there's a nest—so there MUST be a bird—right?)

Do you see a MOUSE?

Spread out on the sofa, close your eyes, and think about what it would be like if you were:
an elephant painting your house with his trunk

a polar bear sitting on top of a skyscraper playing tag with a grizzly bear
having a tea party with an elephant
How about being a big fat pig?
a wiggly worm?
a frog leaping high in the air?
or
a mother cat telling its kittens a story?
Isn't it great to be anything you want to be and do anything you want to do just by closing your eyes?

Look for a puddle of water that's been sitting several days.
Move up very close to see what's going on in it.
You'll be surprised.

Go to your dad, who's so tired after coming home from work but
doesn't he still like to pick you up,
swirl you around
and

tell you you're the most wonderful kid in the whole world?
Does he tell you how much he loves the drawing you made for him and that he's going to show it to Grandma?
Does it seem like he's just smothering you with hugs and kisses, even as he holds you on his lap or lets you sit close beside him? (Don't you love to hear a story this way?)
When you hide behind a chair or a door, does he hunt for you all over the house as if he didn't know where you were—but he really does!
Do you love the tons of attention you get, just as if there were nobody in the world as important as you? Doesn't this make you feel better inside than getting expensive toys?

Walk along the grass.
Is something hopping all around? Try to catch it!
Oops—it got away!
Do you know what insect it was?
It was a grasshopper.
It isn't easy to catch a grasshopper, because the grasshopper is a famous jumper.
The grasshopper can jump like lightning to escape people and birds—birds that would devour it in a flash!
BUT—if you DO capture a grasshopper, you MUST see how hard it works scrubbing and keeping itself very clean.
Watch and you'll see!
(Then—you'll let it fly away, won't you?)

Go to see the burned-out house down the block.
(Doesn't it look so sad?)

Listen.
Do you hear a quiet tapping sound on your window?
What could it be?
Is it a leaf telling you a secret?

Put on your mother's high heels and pretend you are a model.
(Don't those high heels make you feel grown-up?
BUT
Aren't you glad you don't have to wear high heels all day?)

Someday, if you can—
Take an elevator to the top of a tall building—and when you're at the top:
See the whole world around you.
Do people below look like little bugs?
and
Do cars look like the little toy cars you play with?

Put an overripe banana on the ground and just watch to see which insects show up.

Think of some things that give you a good feeling.
Can smelling your favorite flower give you a good feeling?
Can climbing a tree?
What about cuddling your cat?
Wouldn't you love walking along a stream?
How about eating your favorite dessert?
When you play with your good friend?
Do you like it when someone says, "You did a good job of setting the table"?
Does it make you feel good when someone says you're smart?
How about when Grandma says, "I love you"?

Go to your "junk" box and tinker around with anything you feel like tinkering around with. How about:
wheels that came off an old wagon?
old inner tubes?
locks and keys?
jiggly measuring spoons?
squeeze bottles?

berry boxes?
clothespins?
candy boxes?
old wooden spoons?
used postcards?
old pocketbooks?
worn ties?
belts from unwanted clothes?
bottlecaps?
stuffed dolls you had when you were little?

Isn't it great to have a "junk" box? And besides—it's just about the only thing to leave in a mess too!

Play peekaboo with your baby brother.

Put on some music or turn on the radio
AND DANCE AWAY.

Have a "raindrop" race with your brother.
(You never heard of a "raindrop" race before? Well, it's a game children all over the world have played and children will always play—whenever it rains.)

Here's all you have to do:

Each of you pick out a raindrop that's at the top of a window pane
and
the drop that reaches the bottom of the window first wins!

Make some silly pictures by mixing up parts.
Here's how to do it:

Find a picture of a car that has a driver at the wheel.
Cut out the driver at the wheel
and instead—
Paste in a picture of a dog's head.
(Can you keep from laughing?)
Make some other silly pictures.

Listen.

Do you hear the shouts and squeals of children mixed in with the sounds of the trees rustling in the wind as you pass a neighborhood playground?
Together—don't they make a happy sound?

Hunt for a stick.

A stick can do many wonderful things for you:
You can drag a stick.
You can drop a stick and pick it up as many times as you want.
You can draw on earth or sand with a stick.
You can ride a horse on a stick.
A stick is just right for smacking a snow-covered tree.
Supposing a ball went on the other side of a fence,
you might get the ball back with a stick.
You can draw pictures on the snow with a stick.
A stick can be used to lead an orchestra.
And, of course—a stick can be used as a drumstick.
How good are you at hitting stones with a stick—is it something like hitting a golf ball?
Can you make a stockade for wild horses from a lot of little sticks?
Do you have a dog? Then, throw the stick far out and let your dog bring it back to you.
If you need a sword
a trumpet
or
a witch's broom
a stick is just right.
A stick can be a cane, especially good to keep you company along a mountain path—and it makes you feel so good. (If you find a stick that has a nice big knot in it, do you know that it can be a stick with a nose?)
Also, if you have an itch on your back, is there anything better than to scratch it with a stick?
Be the first on your street to make a path after a snowfall. Then find a twig and write your name near the path so that everyone will know who made it.

Make "chocolate" pudding from water poured on soil.
It will be sweet, soft, and yummy for your dolls and dinosaurs
or
How about chicken soup of sand and water for them?

Ask if you can eat your lunch backward so that you can have
your dessert first,
your sandwich next,
and your milk
and
then—your bowl of soup.
How would you like that?

Watch the cat go under the porch when it rains.
Did you ever see a bird tuck its head under its wings when it rains?
A bee would go back to its hive when it rains, wouldn't it?
Wouldn't it be easy to be a turtle when it rains—
how convenient to have a shell to get under.
Cows just stand and get good and wet.
What do you do when it rains?

Play catch with your dad
and then have a cold drink under a shady tree.

Climb up a hill so you can look at faraway places.
Then after a while
See how fast you can roll down the hill.

Go to the zoo.
See the bears ambling back and forth
back and forth
back and forth
(Don't they look awfully bored?)
But WAIT!
The zookeeper is putting a special treat high up on a tree.

A BEAR IS CLIMBING UP TO GET IT!
Look at the prairie dogs.
Don't they look like jack-in-the-boxes as they peek in and out of their underground passages?
Aren't the little egrets cute?
Why are the elks all standing together on top of that high craggy rock?
Do they want to make sure they don't miss anything special that's going on?
Look at those lions chasing each other.
Are they mad at each other or just showing off for us?
Look at those clambering monkeys.
Now they've stopped to eat. (Aren't you glad you came at feeding time?)
Is there a special section of the zoo that is just for fish and turtles and sea horses?
(Don't some of those big fish look like monsters?)
Is there a goldfish or a duck pond so you can feed them the breadcrumbs you brought with you?
Is there a "children's section" for petting rabbits?
Are you tired now? Don't you think it's just about time to go home?

Go for a tandem bicycle ride with your mother.
Can you ride along a path through a park? It's such a special treat, isn't it?

See if you can borrow a pogo stick from one of your friends.
Once you learn to balance yourself on a pogo stick, it's such fun jumping in the air. (But, of course, you always have to be very careful!)

Get some of your friends together to act out some of your favorite stories like:
"Aladdin and His Lamp"
"Cinderella"
"Pinocchio"
"Peter Pan"
"The Pied Piper of Hamelin"
"Alice's Adventures in Wonderland"
What other favorites would you like to act out?

See who in the family can think of the most things you can do with a wheelbarrow.
Then—get out the wheelbarrow and try out some of them.
(Wouldn't it be great to get a ride in a wheelbarrow?)

Put rubberbands (big ones, fat ones, skinny ones) around an open shoe box
and
play guitar.

Go with your grandfather to watch the high school baseball game. (If it's football or basketball season, try to go to these too.)

Ask a grown-up to hang a ball from a tree limb. Swat the ball with a paper towel tube.

Watch your neighbor hanging the wash and singing.
Isn't it nice to hear people singing while they work?

Discover a whole new world with a magnifying glass.
Look carefully at a leaf.
Do you see little veins in it?
Look at a bit of earth. Now do you see why you hear people say that our soil is made up of tiny pieces of stone and rock that wind and water broke up after years
and
years
and
years?
Look closely at:
tree bark
a feather
sand

skin
loose hair
a bud
moss
a dandelion leaf
stamps and coins
water
dirty water from a tin can

See what an ant looks like close-up.

Doesn't a magnifying glass make the tadpole look big?

Float a maple seed in a stream.

If it tangles with anything, just give it a little push.
(Other seeds will float well, too.)

Can you make up new words to the tune "Row, Row, Row Your Boat"?
(Don't get too silly now!)

Look! It's snowing outside!

Watch the snowflakes
floating down
swirling
and
dancing in the streets.

Go out and feel the snow. Is it light and powdery?

See how the snow covers houses,
trees
and
everything, turning the world into a fairyland.

How tall can you build a tower from blocks of snow?

Take a walk in the snow and then follow your footsteps all the way back.

Go sledding up and down the hillside.

(Isn't it wonderful that all this snow, all this snow that came down to us—came so quietly? You never heard a snowflake make a sound when it dropped to the ground—did you?)

Be a scientist and find out which of these things will float in water and those that won't:

a walnut shell
a metal spoon
a plastic foam container
How about a block of wood?
Do you have a cork? Will it float?

Think of what you'd rather be than you—
Would you rather be
a zookeeper?
a quarterback?
a homemaker?
a great prince?
a giant?
the president of the United States?
Well—maybe after all—it's just best to be YOU!

Give this some thought:
Some people live in big houses and have lots of things.
Some people live in little houses and don't have a lot of things.
It's how you are inside that counts.

Some people are Catholic.
Some people are Protestant.
Some people are Jewish.
It's how you are inside that counts.

Some people are brown.
Some people are yellow.
Some people are reddish brown.
Some people are white.
Some people are shades lighter or darker.
It's how you are inside that counts.

Some people are teachers.
Some people work in a gasoline station.
Some people work in a factory.
Some people don't have a job.
  It's how you are inside that counts.

Some people are strong.
Some people are sick.
Some people are blind.
Some people are crippled.
  It's how you are inside that counts.

Some people are Polish.
Some people are Italian.
Some people are Nigerian.
Some people are Colombian.
  It's how you are inside that counts.

What are the things that count?
  Can people depend on you? Do you do what you say you'll do?
  Do you always try to tell the truth?
  Are you friendly to people?
  Do you go out of your way to help people?

Enjoy the precious smells of the herb garden.
  Do you know that peppermint gum uses the peppermint herb?
  Do you know that the furniture polish fragrance is taken from lemon balm?
    and that
  The mouth-watering aroma of our lentil soup comes from parsley?

Make up something—anything that rhymes with a person's name—like:
  "Mark, Mark went to the park."
  "Paul, Paul is very tall."
  "Ellen, Ellen likes watermelon."

Now make up some of your own!

Walk down the street and look at the oldest houses there—
Look at their old worn-out steps.
Does it make you think about the
hundreds
and
hundreds
of footsteps that wore into them through the years?
Do you think some children played "school" on those steps?

Have a friend guess what animal you are pretending to be.
Give just one hint, like:
I like to nibble leaves at the very top. (giraffe)
My picture is on money. (eagle)
People say I move slowly. (turtle)
Listen to me talk. (parrot)
My bill holds lots of fish. (pelican)
I am large, white, and graceful. (swan)
Your coat may come from me. (sheep)
Farmers try to scare me. (crow)
My arms are built for swinging. (monkey)
I am a sly one. (fox)
I am a symbol of peace. (dove)

Draw a picture of a tree.
If you're right-handed, draw the tree with your left hand.
If you're left-handed, draw the tree with your right hand.
Isn't the difference interesting?
Does it make you wonder "why"?

Go outdoors and watch the sun sinking in the west
and
watch the birds going home to their nests.
Listen to the whippoorwill.
(You'll probably never forget her song.)
Do you hear the crow "caw-cawing," saying "good night" to you?

On a sunny day—
See the shadows that are made.
Look at the trees' shadows.
Even the porch railing makes shadows—
and
the fire hydrant.
Dogs make shadows
and
birds
and
insects,
flowers
and
YOU!
Can your fingers make shadow pictures?
Can you step on your shadow?
Do you know how to play "Shadow Tag"?
In "Shadow Tag," you don't tag the person.
You're supposed to JUMP on the person's shadow!
Try it—it's lots of fun!

Find out a little bit more about this great, wonderful world we live in. How much your fingers can tell you!
Touch shells—are some ripply? are some smooth?
Do all pebbles feel the same?
Did you ever feel corn silk?
Have you touched ice-cold water? steamy hot water?
water that is just right for your bath?
Does rabbit's fur feel like your kitten's?
Did you ever feel prickly pine needles?

Think about some things that go up and down—
Things like:
elevators
birds
What else?

Stop your running, jumping, and playing to do some things that would please your mother or father.

If your driveway is messy, can you brush or sweep the mess away? (It's better to do it this way than hosing it down because hosing it wastes gallons and gallons of water. You want to help save the Earth, don't you?)

Can you sweep the kitchen floor?

Can you help set the table all by yourself? (Listen to the tinkle of the dishes as the table is being set. Isn't it a pretty sound?)

Do you know where the dishes and silverware go? and how to fold napkins—and where to put them?

Can you husk the corn and shell the peas all by yourself?

What about the dirty dishes? Can you scrape them and bring them to the sink for washing and drying? (Notice all the bubbles there are in the water! Doesn't it look like a bubble mountain?)

Do you think your mother would be pleased if you ate up your whole sandwich AND the crust?

Do you think she would be especially pleased if you went to your bed after lunch and took a nice long nap—ALL BY YOURSELF?

Think about this:

If all flowers were buttercups instead of roses
sunflowers
or
tulips

If all the birds were robins instead of swallows
peacocks
or
hummingbirds

If all the animals were turtles, elephants,
or
camels

If everyone looked all the same instead of tall
short
fat
or
thin

If all names were Smith instead of Olinski
Angelo
or
Ayad

If everyone were Protestant instead of Jewish
Muslim
or
Catholic

If all people lived in houses like yours instead of igloos
big apartments
or
pueblos

If everyone were a doctor instead of a construction worker
sanitation worker
or
teacher

WHAT A DULL WORLD IT WOULD BE!

Take a close peek at the pansy growing in a garden.

Doesn't it look like a face?

Do you see the eyes?

a nose?

and

a mouth?

Doesn't it have a pretty face?

See that house they're building down the block? It's just about all done, and they have a pile of extra bricks.

Find out if they will let you have a few so that you can build a house too.

See how long you can stand on one foot.

Start making a button collection. Parents, grandparents, neighbors, and friends will be glad to help you out.

Think of all the things you can do with a button collection! You can:

Swirl them around and around.

Pick out the buttons you like best.

Can you sort out the metal buttons, the ones you use for jeans?

Do you have any buttons that were used for shoes a long time ago?

Sort into piles buttons that have:

four holes

three holes

two holes

one hole

NO holes

Sort the buttons into piles of

small

medium

and

big ones

Can you sort the buttons by color?

Which color do you have the most of? the least of?

Are you lucky enough to have any buttons made from seashells?

Can you write your name with buttons?
Can you make a necklace by stringing buttons together?
Lay out buttons and make roadways with them.
How many buttons can you toss into an empty oatmeal box or a hat?

Flip through the newspaper to the comics section—
Cut out each picture of your favorite comic strip.
Mix up all the pictures.
And—then see if you can put them together in the same order as they were in before.

* You can do the same thing with an old picture book.
** Make up your own story with pictures you draw, mix them up, and put THEM together in the same order.

Sit in your rocking chair and "take off" on a visit to faraway places:
Visit China and Japan.
Take a boat ride on the Mississippi River.
Go on a caravan in the desert.
Wouldn't it be fun to go to the North Pole?

Discuss with grown-ups which of these things pollute our earth, and why or why not.
skating?
TV?
hiking?
a bicycle?
a motorboat?
a canoe, sailboat, or rowboat?
an airplane?
walking?
reading a book?
a videocassette?
a refrigerator?
cars?
a campfire?
an electric stove?

Start a collection of stones. Stones can be found anywhere:
in a streambed
by the ocean
on mountains and hills
in the city—anywhere!

Look for stones that are
smooth
rough
grainy
gritty
glassy
scratchy
sparkly
roundish or squarish
flat or fat

Besides enjoying the beauty of stones, look at all the things you can do with a stone:

You can throw a stone so that it skips
one
two
or
more times
across a pond.

You can drop a stone in water and marvel as it spirals downward.

You can press on a hard stone and see how its hardness seems to press on you.

You can try to use a big hard stone as a hammer and a chopper (that's how people a long, long time ago ground grain for making bread).

You can kick a stone all the way down the block—and around it too.

You can use a pretty stone for a paperweight.

You can fill a basket with pretty stones just to look at.

There are a lot more things you can do with a stone.

BUT ONE THING YOU MUST NEVER DO IS THROW STONES AT PEOPLE.

Do you know the word that tells you what these helpers are?
the person who fixes your teeth when they hurt you
the person who puts out fires
the person who gives you a health checkup
the person who helps you pick out books to read
the person who sees that cars don't go too fast
the person who helps you cross the street

Pretend you are a daisy opening up to the sky when the sun comes out after a gentle rain.

While you're eating your breakfast—
Look out at the morning glories in your garden
and
Listen to the robin sing on the branch of the apple tree.
Don't they seem happy that it's spring?
Aren't you too?

Watch what happens when the tire on the car runs over a big piece of glass. Look carefully.
Doesn't the tire look as if it's melting?

Stroll around your neighborhood just to see what you can see. (If it's cold out, try to stay in the sunny areas to stay warmer.)

Which of these do you see?
Children roller-skating?
A mother or father with a baby carriage?
Trees reaching up to the sky?
Someone sprinkling a lawn?
shaking out a mop?
cleaning windows?
A traffic cop?
Children coming home from school?
Some people walking?
jogging?
Old and young people?
The neighborhood food market?
A flag waving in the breeze?
Old and new houses?
big and little houses?
apartment houses?
A dog wagging its tail?
A mother calling her child in for lunch?
Is that your friend waving to you from her window?

African Americans? Native Americans? Hispanic Americans? Asian Americans? European Americans?

Isn't it wonderful to see people of different skin color? Isn't it a little like a pretty bouquet of flowers?

Go with a grown-up to a friendly gas station and get permission to watch

how customers get different kinds of gas. Hear them say:
"Fill it up, please."
or
"Five dollars worth of unleaded gas, please."

See how the gas is pumped in and watch the meter that says the tank is filled up.

Watch how air is put in tires and how a flat tire is repaired.

Best of all, isn't it fun to see how the mechanic can lift up the car and work on its underside?

Speak into an empty oatmeal box and touch the bottom lightly with your fingertips.

Can you feel it giving off
a kind of humming,
a gentle vibration?

Play with your pet. Which pet do you have:

ants?
a cat? a dog?
chickens?
a cricket?
gerbils?
a rabbit?
a grasshopper?
a canary? a parakeet?
a snake (a harmless one, of course)
tadpoles?
a turtle?
a caterpillar?
goldfish?
guinea pigs?
a lizard?
minnows?
a snail?
a spider?
any worms?
a frog?

(Don't frogs make the funniest croaking sound you ever heard in your whole life?)

hamsters?

(Have you ever wondered why your hamster likes your pocket and the inside of your blouse so much?)

Aren't pets great for loving
and
just watching "when there's nothing special to do"?

Bob around and sing along to Pete Seeger or Woody Guthrie songs.
Songs like:

"Put Your Finger in the Air"
"I Love My Rooster"
"Clean-O-Clean"
"Wake Up"
or
"May There Always Be Sunshine"

Do any of your friends have other music? If not, borrow some from your library.

If you have a great big, empty apple cider jar—
Use it to start a penny collection and watch it grow.
Uppps! Is that a penny on the sidewalk?
(What a great beginning!)

Watch the man shoveling lots of coal from his truck down a coal chute—
into a building.
Lots of grown-ups like to watch this too—and even dogs. One day you may want to get permission to see where that coal is being dumped—and why.

Figure out three things you can do with these scraps and leftovers:

empty spools of thread
plastic lids
jars
ice cream sticks
window shades
wire hangers
plastic foam meat trays
newspapers
sponges
cans
noodles
aluminum foil
puzzle pieces
shells
combs
forks

empty paper bags
wire mesh
inner tubes
old socks, stockings
fur
rugs
nuts and bolts
safety pins
washers
heavy twine
yarn
burlap
leather scraps
all kinds of material
old sheets
construction paper
tissue
cellophane
cardboard
shelf paper
pebbles
bottlecaps
wax paper
bones
rice
clothespins
bark
brushes
rubber bands
felt
netting
rickrack
dried flowers
seeds
photos
buttons
matchboxes
playing cards
gift wrapping
linoleum scraps
metal pieces
plastic scraps
wrapping paper
corrugated cardboard
screws

Think of one, two, or three things you can learn from:
worms
wagons
a fallen feather
running against the wind
bumps
—even the sniffles!

Admire your little pussycat.
When you call her name to come and eat, she comes.
If she spills any of her milk, she knows how to lick it up.
She knows how to clean herself with her tongue, doesn't she? (And you don't have to tell her to either!)
If she's unhappy about something, she'll cry—oh, so sadly. It's almost enough to make you cry too.

If you have a ball of yarn or a sock filled with cotton, she'll play with it for hours if you let her.

If you have to be away and leave her with a neighbor, the neighbor won't mind because cats are easier to take care of than dogs, which usually want to go outside, run, and such things.

Cats really understand children. Yours knows when you're happy or sad.

When you're sad, she'll come to you, look you sadly in your eyes, and say, "I'm with you."

If you're very busy and you don't want her around, you just say "scat" and she'll go away.

When she wants to go out, she lets you know. When she wants to come back in, she lets you know that too. (But don't bother following her when she goes out. THAT'S HER SECRET.)

Cats are fun

BUT

You mustn't do anything to hurt a cat (like pulling her by her tail)—or she'll SCRATCH!

Sit on the porch swing
with the wind whispering you a lullaby
until you fall asleep.

Is that the balloon man coming down the street?
Get out your penny collection and buy one.
What color will you get—red? blue? yellow?

Go visit Grandma and Grandpa.

Besides a lot of loving, aren't they good for:

Baking delicious homemade blueberry pie?

(Does Grandma let you help roll out the crust for the pie

and

sample the whipped cream to make sure it's just right?)

Does Grandma let down hems for dresses and jeans when they are too short?

and

when you have holes in your socks, does Grandma darn them for you?

Would Grandpa like to play a game of checkers with you?
(He's pretty sharp for his age, isn't he?)
Do they dance any of these dances they danced when they were younger—like:
the "Charleston"?
the "Jitterbug"?
a jig
or
the "Twist"?
How about a game of dominoes. Does Grandpa like to play this game with you? If he's too tired, would Grandma?
Do you like to snuggle close together on the sofa for stories about when they were little?
Do you think that Grandma and Grandpa are also the best babysitters in the whole world?

Play in your treehouse with some of your friends.
Do you think Mother would be able to serve lunch for all of you up there?

Take a long, hard look at that tree stump that everyone wants to get rid of.
Do you know that this tree stump is not just a stump?
The stump is a seat you can sit on.
You can fill the stump with soil and flowers in the summertime, and everyone will come to the stump to look at it.
In the winter you can fill the stump with evergreen boughs.
The stump can make a good base for a sundial.
You can make a fine piece of sculpture from mud, and the stump can be a base for it.
Or
How about setting a special birdhouse on top of the stump.
Do you know that a stump is just what you need when Dad wants to show you how to hammer nails into a piece of wood?
BUT—
THE VERY BEST THING ABOUT A STUMP IS THAT YOU CAN CLIMB ON TOP OF IT AND BE THE STRONGEST, BRAVEST PERSON IN THE WORLD!

(P.S.—If you really have to get rid of the stump—ask the stump grinder to make it into a pile of wood chips so you can mulch the garden.)

In the cold, winter months,
when snow covers the ground
and you long for the sight of spring—
why not gather twigs from the pussywillow bushes
and put them in water on a sunny windowsill.
(With water and warmth the buds will open.)

Wiggle each toe of your baby sister with:
"This little piggy went to market."
"This little piggy stayed home."
"This little piggy had roast beef."
"This little piggy had none."
"This little piggy cried 'Wee Wee Wee' all the way home."

Find an empty tin can.
Does it make a noise when it drops?
Does your voice sound the same when you shout into it?
Does it reflect light like a mirror when you take the paper off?
Can you put pebbles or beans in it
and
then
shake
shake
shake?

Take a trip to the local animal shelter. You may be lucky enough to see some new puppies,
a big fluffy cat,
or
a noisy parrot.
Just what is that noisy parrot trying to say?
Does he want you to take him home with you?

Play a hopping game with your friend.
See who can hop in place the longest without putting the other foot on the ground.
Or
Hop around with the arms folded and see who goes farther.

Go to the circus or carnival that comes to town.
(If you can't—can you line up with crowds of people on the curb to watch the circus parade march down your main street?)

Do you see children with colorful balloons? (Can you get one too?)
Do you hear the big brass band?
What silly things the clowns do!
Isn't it thrilling to watch people on the trapeze fly through the air? Doesn't it look so dangerous too?
Don't the elephants look silly all dressed up?
Watch those snakes going in and out of everything.
Aren't the floats so fancy and so pretty?
Look at the monkeys doing their tricks.
Watch the camels and ponies and donkeys and chariots with horses.
Listen to the people screaming their heads off. (You too!)

(Do you think you'll ever forget this circus or the parade?)

* If you can't go to the circus or watch the parade—perhaps you'll be able to watch the tents being set up and taken down.

This is lots of fun too—maybe even more fun than watching the show itself!

Watch the street-cleaning truck as it comes slowly down the street!
SWISSHH! SWISSHH! SWISSHH!

Get all your friends behind you
And all of you waddle like ducks.

See how high you can build a card tower with a deck of cards.

Be a tightrope walker.
See how far you can walk down a long chalk line without taking your feet off the line
and
without "falling" off it.

Listen to:
Peter and the Wolf by Prokofiev
Carnival of the Animals by Saint-Saëns
Mother Goose Suite by Ravel
Toy Symphony by Haydn
Nutcracker Suite by Tchaikovsky
Petrouchka by Stravinsky
Peer Gynt by Grieg
The Sorcerer's Apprentice by Dukas

* If you don't own these recordings, do you have a library so you can borrow them? You'll love the stories and you can dance to them too!

Rummage through some old unused things in the trunk in the attic.
Look—there's a music box!
Wind it up
and then
sing along to its pretty tune.

Have a hilarious time by taking some words and making them rhyme. Just pick out things that have the same sound, like:
Buy a cat that isn't fat.
Find a snail and put it in a pail.
Can you make one up about a fly and a pie?

Make yourself look and act as if you were as still as a great mountain and as powerful as thunder.
(It *can* be done—try it!)

Think about how lucky we are to have noses—
to get whiffs of
the vanilla in chocolate chip cookies
the fruitiness of jellies, tarts, and jams
angel food cake
cotton candy
chicken soup
fruit pies
UMMMMMMMM!

Play an old, old rhyming game.
It goes like this:
How many words can you think of that rhyme with
"and" (band, hand, sand, etc.)
"at"
"all"
"red"

Take a pretend trip.

A box or shopping bag can be your suitcase to pack your clothes in as you get ready.
Cut out magazine pictures of places you want to go.
Make your own tickets from pieces of paper or cardboard.
Line up some chairs for a train or bus
AND OFF YOU GO!

Get the empty shoe box and cut out windows and a door.
Paint it red—and it becomes a red barn for a farm.
If you eat your lunch next to it, you can pretend you are picnicking at the farm.
What else can you make from a shoe box?

Think of five words or more that rhyme with:
"an"
"in"
"all"
What about
"ump"?

You and Mother take a bus instead of the car and visit a friend.
Bus rides are good for looking out the window to see:
people
houses
stores
trees and flowers and beautiful things of nature.
Bus rides are also good for:
talking together
telling jokes
holding hands
and
not having to worry about traffic
and other dangerous things.
(Sometimes you can even take a tiny snooze on your mother's shoulder on a bus ride.)

On a very hot day, notice how the asphalt of your driveway gets soft, and how on a cold day, it gets hard again.
Can you figure out why?
If you can't, ask someone who might know. You can learn a lot if you ask questions. Some of the greatest people asked a lot of questions!

Play "car wash" with bicycles
tricycles
wagons
rags for washing and drying them
and
a bucket of water.
(Be sure to make them shine.)

Take an early morning walk in the woods when the sparkling drops of dew cover the ground.
See how the old long, shiny pine needles make a carpet on the ground.

Look for acorns fallen from the oak trees. (Be sure to take some home for the squirrels who live near you.)

Do you see footprints that look like tiny hands? Those belong to the raccoon.

See if you can find a turtle sitting on a rock in the water. Turtles like to bask in the sun.

Do you hear rat-a-tat-tat-ing? Those are woodpeckers tapping trees with their beaks, looking for insects to eat.

If you see a tree with a hanging nest—it's probably the home of a beautiful oriole.

Can you stay longer and sit beside a fire? You'd be able to hear the crickets chirping and the frogs croaking.

It would be the end of a beautiful, beautiful day!

Visit an aquarium to see all kinds of water animals, like:

whales
octopuses
sea lions
dolphins
sea horses
starfish

Do you think they mind swimming in circles all day?
Do you think some of them ever get homesick for the ocean?

(If it's a foggy day)

Walk down the block a little way.
Have you ever wondered what fog is?
You've seen clouds that are high up in the sky—haven't you?
Well, fog is just a cloud that is resting on the ground.

Isn't it interesting to think of how much your dog is able to "say" without talking the way we do?

When your dog makes little barks, wags his tail, and the tail goes up in the air, he's telling you he's happy—isn't he?

When your dog wants to let you know he loves you, does he leap up, lick you with his tongue, and kiss your nose?

If there is a strange person around and he wants to let it be known he's a friendly dog—will he sniff?

When your dog is afraid of something or someone, does he crawl away?

What makes your dog howl and growl and show his teeth? Is he saying that something or someone isn't pleasing him?
(That's good for protecting your house—isn't it?)

Touch the groceries that were just unpacked from shopping.
Feel the squash
Feel the watermelon
Feel the tomatoes
apples
grapefruit
potatoes
onion
etc.
Each feels so different. Did you ever think about that?

Play a "Hiding Game."
In a "Hiding Game" children take turns hiding something, like a ball, a key, or a bottletop.
Then the one who hid the object calls "cold"
"lukewarm"
"very warm"
"very hot"
"BURNING"
as the other children move closer to the object when they look for it.

Go someplace where you can see horses—a farm or maybe a riding stable.

See how fast horses can run.
Doesn't it look as if the horses have more than four legs? They almost seem impossible to count!
Watch how the horses trot
and
See how gracefully horses jump over bars.
Watch how horses eat their hay—
chewing
and
chewing
and
chewing!
Keep your eyes on a horse's tail. You'll know that a horse is smart, the way he uses his tail to swat flies away!
Wouldn't you love to take a ride on a horse someday?

Hang old keys or measuring spoons on a piece of string.
Hang them in a breezy place
and
Listen to the music of your wind chimes.

Look at a snowflake through a magnifying glass.
Can you count the number of sides on each snowflake?
Do you know that every single snowflake has six sides?
Each snowflake is different—but each snowflake has six sides!

Think of all the great things your two feet can do:
You can:
walk with your feet
run
jump
skip
hop
dance
and
make "feet" tracks in the snow.
What else?

Just think about "wheels"—how wonderful they are for people.

What are some things that have wheels?

bicycles?
tricycles?
wagons?
big wheels on a sanitation truck?
bigger wheels on a road grader?
car wheels?

Did you ever see the wheel of a Ferris wheel at a carnival?
Would you like to go high in the sky on one of those wheels?

See how many spools of thread
buttons or
popcorn
you can drop into the hole you have cut in the lid of a shoe box.
Can you count the ones you dropped in?

Plant some morning glory seeds in a sunny spot beside your fence and watch how the plants climb up the fence.

Do you know why this flower is called "morning glory"—instead of "afternoon glory"? Take a look at your plants in the morning and then in the afternoon. That will tell you the answer!

Visit a botanical garden.
It's glorious in the fall
and great in the winter.
In the spring it's super
BUT IN THE SUMMER—well—you just have to be there for—
the smell of flowers!
the bulbs in full bloom!
the forest and meadows alive with wildflowers!

Make a "one-minute" ball by squashing a piece of newspaper into a ball.

This ball won't bounce, but it's very good for tossing into a basket. (It's also good because it can't hurt little children.)

Can you imagine what a wonderful sight it would be to find butterflies dancing in a falling snow!

Go swinging on a swing.
Doesn't it make you feel like a bird in the sky?
Can you reach a cloud?

Go skating.
Fly!
Whiz by little children.
Swing around the corner.
How long can you skate on one skate and not fall down?

Watch your favorite bird.
What can you find out about your bird?
Do you know its color or colors?
Do you know how it flies?
What it likes to eat and when?
Have you seen its nest?
Have you ever seen its eggs and babies?
Do you know its song?
Can you draw a picture of your bird and post it on the kitchen bulletin board?

Everyone pack into the car to visit a nature farm.
Do they have special hikes to look for plants?
Do they have night hikes to listen to the bats and owls?
Do they have places where you can see beaver dams?
What about snakes? Will they help you find snakes?
Will they let you handle a harmless snake—such as a garter snake?

Set up a lemonade stand for thirsty people who pass your house.

Ask everyone in the family this question:
"What is happiness?"
Are the answers the same?
What is your answer?

Make a butterfly in the snow.
It's very simple. You just lie on your back on a patch of smooth, clean snow
and
Move your arms and legs up and down.
And now you have a butterfly. But you must be very careful when you get up or you'll mar the wings.
If you'd rather make an angel with wings, you can make it the same way.

Go join your old neighbor friend, who is always sitting under the cherry tree in his backyard
and
Listen to him talk about his life long ago—
the work he did
his children
and
his children's
children . . .

Watch that bee dipping in and out of the flowers.
Doesn't the bee always seem to work and never play?
Doesn't the bee know that
"All work and no play makes Jack a dull boy"?

Think of what you would do if you had a pair of wings.
Would you fly across the sky?
glide across the seas?
soar mountain peaks?
Where would you go?

Make a pair of glasses from pipe cleaners.
Make them so that they fit you when you read your bedtime story.

See how sharp you are.
Can you tell when someone is sweeping?
when the bathtub is filling up for someone's bath? Or
is someone taking a shower?
when fresh paint is on the wall?
when someone is broiling fish?
when honeysuckle blossoms are on the vine?
Suppose a ship got caught in a heavy fog—how would you know?
What would you hear?

Play a whirling game with someone bigger and stronger than you who picks you up by your hands and whirls you around and around and around
until you get dizzier and dizzier and dizzier
and then you slow
down
down
down
down!

Visit an animal shelter.
Does it make you feel sad?
But when the animals see you smile at them—your smile will help them feel better.

Take a walk. But you must take a special kind of walk. You must walk or jump over the sidewalk lines onto the next section of sidewalk. Try it!

Get out your collection of bottlecaps and write your name with them.

Can you write your address with them?
your birthday?
What else?

Go see your baby brother. Aren't you glad you are so grown up and can do so many things that he can't do? For example:

Your baby brother is tired most of the day.
You can go out and play and have lots of fun. All you need is just a little nap after lunch.
Your baby brother drinks milk from Mother's breast or from a baby bottle.
You drink milk like grown-ups, from a cup.

Your baby brother messes around with clay and mud and gets it all over himself.
But you know how to make cookies and houses and clean up when you're done.

How your brother scribbles with crayons.
You know how to make pretty pictures.

When your baby brother gets hold of a book, he just crumbles the pages.
But you don't. You like the stories and pictures—don't you?

Baby brothers don't know that it's dangerous to put pins or buttons in the mouth.
You give them to Mother or put them where they belong.

Babies think blocks are for throwing all around.
But you know a million things you can build with blocks because you're so BIG!

What else can you do that your baby brother can't do—yet!

Go on a blindfold walk in your backyard and just touch.

Can you tell if you are touching:
a tree?
a flower?

a feather?
twigs?
an earthworm?
a tomato?
a garage?
the fence?
What about the blocks that are scattered all over the yard that you didn't put away?

Look outside—quick!
See a cat trying to catch a rat . . .
P O U N C E! prrrrr

Listen to the different sounds you can make just by tapping.
For example:
Listen to the sounds of the taps when you tap different parts of a metal pot
a table
or
a refrigerator.
Do they make different sounds when you tap with different things, like
a pencil?
a spoon?
or
a penny?

Get out the grapefruit seeds you saved from your breakfast and make a grapefruit forest.
All you need to start your forest are:
some grapefruit seeds
some baby food jars
a little bit of soil
And all you need to do is:
Put some soil in the baby food can
Put the seeds just a little bit in the soil
Cover with a little bit of soil
Keep it wettish
(When green shoots come up in about two weeks, put the jar in a sunny window.)

Look for a worm after a rain.
(Hungry birds are smart and are on the lookout too for worms!)
Some children like to scare other children by teasing them with worms. But there are a lot of nicer things you can do with worms.
You can watch the worms and see how they move about by getting
longer and thinner
and
shorter and fatter.
Pick up a worm and feel its soft, moist body.
You can watch the worm in the apple you almost ate.
When you're finished playing with and watching the worm, put it back in the earth so it can continue to do its work.

Make a train of empty shoe boxes strung together with string
and
Go from "city" to "city" about the house.

Set yourself down on the ground and keep your eyes open for ants.
Do you find one dragging a great big crumb?
Follow an ant all the way to where it's going.
(Aren't its feet tiny? Can you imagine what it must feel like to have such tiny feet? But ants do get around to a lot of places—even places where people don't want them!)
See if you can find an ant climbing a blade of grass.
Can you get an ant to climb up your finger? (It tickles, doesn't it?)
Isn't it interesting that ants don't seem to be afraid of people even though they're so tiny. We must look like giants to them!
Ants must have wonderful noses too. Just think—a tiny ant can probably smell your mother's cake better than you can!

Make a painting of anything in this whole world you like.
You don't have a paintbrush? Then paint with:
a toothbrush
an old hairbrush

the tip of a feather
pine needles
toothpicks
cut-up sponges
string
your fingertips.

You don't have regular artist's paper to paint on? Then try:

old newspapers
flattened paper bags
or
the ripply side of a cardboard carton
some unwanted wallpaper samples.

(Remember that steps
sidewalks
refrigerators
and
fences are just right for painting with water.)

Plop yourself on a chair and watch what someone else is doing.

(Sometimes it's nice to do just that AND NO MORE! Isn't that so?)

If you're up late at night, get out your flashlight, go into your garden, and hunt for a slug.

Is that one nibbling on leaves?

See how it eats and eats and eats.

(It just never seems to ever stop eating. Doesn't it seem that the slug could eat up just about everything in the whole garden? Now you know why slugs usually do their eating at night—WHEN NOBODY'S AROUND!)

When you're in the country—

Follow a crooked brook as far as you can.

Wouldn't it be just wonderful to be able to launch a toy boat or a leaf in the brook through towns, states, and countries—all the way to the ocean!

See if you and your parents can visit a huge planting of lilacs when they're in full bloom.
Or perhaps
you can visit a special azalea planting when they are at their showiest.

Jump as high as you can.
Can you jump backward?
forward?
sideways?
jump and turn about in the air?
jump and clap your hands?
jump and land as quietly as possible?

Collect old cans.
Be a great recycler by re-using your cans.
Turn them into:
vases for flowers
pencil holders
trucks
and
banks

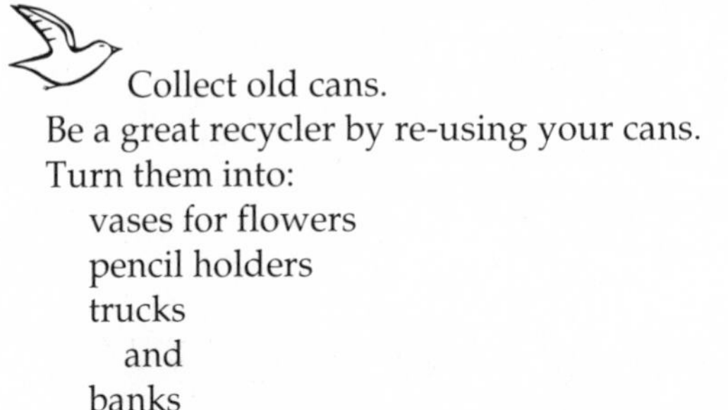

If you have cans left over, you can put them out on recycling day.

Do you think people who love:
mosses
wildflowers
the streams
and
trees
and people
would toss cans about?

Play in your homemade playground of:
truck tires

wooden boxes
long planks
a low ladder
wooden tubs
plastic molasses buckets
rope
a sawhorse
hollow blocks

Don't you think you can have as much fun in your homemade playground (maybe even more!) as in a store-bought one?

Lie on your back and watch the clouds.
Do you see any that look like
woolly sheep?
a rabbit?
or
a ghost?
Wouldn't you love to go floating on a cloud over the whole world?

Make a "sandpile" of cornmeal or oatmeal in a big metal baking pan or a plastic dishpan.
Get out a sieve
a funnel
spoons
and
measuring spoons
and have a great time!

Get to know your pet canary a little bit more.
Does she like to talk to you?
Did you notice that when she goes to sleep she tucks her head under her wing for the night and looks like a little ball of feathers on the perch?
Can you tell by her songs if she's:
lonely?
hungry?
very happy?
frightened?

when she's scolding you?
Do you like her singing voice and the way she throws her head back and looks like a great opera star?
Can you hum along with your canary?

Sit on the back porch and just wonder about things like:
What is the light?
the dark?
the moon?
the rain?
a fallen leaf?
Are they nature's messengers calling you to pay attention to them?
What are the clouds—where do they go, what do they do when they're finished sailing through the sky?
What happened to the dream you dreamed last night?
Most people like the summer more than the winter—
BUT
in the winter
You can see the bare, strong shape of the trees.
You can see the birds' nests in them better.
You can see the knot-holes on their trunks.
You can see how the leaves have drifted onto the fencerows.
The winds are roaring and gusting.
The snow lies deep on the earth.
And the whole world is there for you to enjoy.
Why does the little living, crooked plant you grew all by yourself mean so much to you—maybe even a lot more than some cut flowers someone bought you?
I wonder . . .

Help make a real go-cart.
It would have to have a kind of steering wheel, rubber wheels, and—of course—a seat for rides.
(Did you ever, in your wildest dreams, imagine that you would have a real go-cart all your own?)

After a rain—look down along curbstones or as you go along places where cars have been.

Do you see gasoline "rainbows" in the puddles?
(Even though we don't like to see gasoline spilled, the "rainbows" are pretty—aren't they?)

Visit the old woman who lives alone down the street.
Isn't she nice to give you a daffodil in the spring
or
a cookie she has just baked?
And she always smiles at you and waves her hand when you pass by. Sometimes she even throws you a kiss too.

Help plant marigolds in your vegetable garden.
Do you know that their very strong smell keeps garden pests away from the vegetables?
Aren't they really wonderful garden guards
and
They're so pretty too!

Hunt for a four-leaf clover.
But, if you find a three-leaf clover
and
if it's blooming
bend down
get close to the flowers
and
you'll smell one of the sweetest perfumes in the world!

* If you should want a super bonus treat, taste clover honey!

Go in the backyard and pick up the pail that was upside-down.
Then watch the snail that slept there overnight come out. Doesn't she look like she's raring to go?

Think about the snail. You really have to admire this tiny character.
Just think of all the remarkable things it can do, some things that even you can't do:
The snail can carry his home on his back, and he carries it wherever he goes too!

If anyone dares to want to hurt him, all he has to do is tuck himself inside his house—and he's safe.
He can climb over rocks—and, to think that a rock can be like a mountain to us!
Can you hang from the top of a box or a jar? A snail can!
See how a snail will flip over from his back to his front or from his front to his back. Pretty wonderful—don't you think?
The snail always seems to be relaxed and so easy-going. He's so slow and never, ever seems to be in a hurry. Do you think that sometimes the snail wonders if there's something just not right with some people because they're always in such a hurry?

Look at your mother's hands.
All the wonderful things those hands can do for you! (Did you ever think about it?)
Those beautiful hands can:

bake cookies to munch
tie shoelaces and ribbons
patch a pocket
zip you in and button you up
knit a sweater for you
pat your cheeks
wash dishes
blow kisses and wave good-bye

What can your father's hands do?
What can your hands do?

Make a pair of boxing gloves by stuffing two bags with crumpled paper
putting your hands inside them
and
having someone attach them to your wrist.
Then, have a pretend boxing match with a friend.

Go hunting to see if you can find two stones that are exactly alike.

You won't! Because no two things are ever, ever exactly alike. If you don't think it's so—check it out and you will see that
no two trees are exactly alike
no two flowers are exactly alike
no two birds are exactly alike

AND NO ONE IS EXACTLY LIKE YOU!

Ride your hobbyhorse.
Pretend you are galloping through the fields
the mountains
and
the forest
up and down
up and down
up and down.
Slow down now and stop for some water at the stream.

Make a museum of your own to display your nature collection and things you have made using twigs, seeds, leaves, or other items from nature. You could also show your live pets, like guppies or snakes.
Maybe you would be able to use the empty half of the garage
or
a corner of the back porch.
Don't you think it would be fun for you and would also show your friends how wonderful nature is?

If it's springtime—
See if you can find a crocus.
It just seems that crocus can't wait for the snow to melt to push up its pretty flowers—all ready to greet us after a bitterly cold winter.
"Good morning,
How do you do this fine chilly morning?" say the crocus flowers.

Admire the pretty zinnia and marigold in your backyard.
Just think—

Wouldn't it be great if the summer days never faded away
and
These same pretty flowers could stay forever—
(at least until Thanksgiving?)

Watch flies crawling straight up a wall.
Children can leap
and
dance
and
run
But can they walk straight up a wall like a fly?

Make a xylophone you can use to play a solo,
accompany a soloist,
or
play along with music on the radio.
Just get 3, 4, 5, 6, or more glasses.
Fill each with water, each one with more than the other.
Then, tap the glasses with a spoon and enjoy!

Think of how scrumptious it would be
if lemon drops
fig bars

and
animal crackers
grew on bushes
and you could fill baskets with them
and eat as many as you wanted!

See if you can tell what time it is by the sounds you hear in the house:
What sounds do you hear
before breakfast?
after breakfast?
What sounds do you hear
at lunchtime?
at dinnertime?
at night before you go to sleep?
Do you think you could almost be a clock?

Take a walk in the woods.
Did you find prickly burrs stuck to your pants or socks?
These burrs may seem like a nuisance
BUT
They are hitchhikers (seeds hitching their way on your clothes to a new home).

DON'T THROW THEM AWAY.
You can make all kinds of things with those burrs.
You can make a burr man or woman
or
a burr house
JUST BY STICKING THE BURRS TOGETHER.
OR
Just pick the burrs off your clothes and plant them in the soil.

Show what you do when you're very happy.
Do you clap your hands?
What do you do when you're very sad?
Do you cry?
What do you do when you're very angry?

Do you stamp your feet?
When you're very, very sleepy?
That one's easy. You close your eyes, don't you?

Go take a bath.
Take the kind of bath where it's O.K. if you talk to yourself
or
if you want to sing out loud
or
if you just daydream.
If you want to splash—nobody will mind (except if it gets to be too splashy).
If you put a piece of paper in the water, you can see what happens to the paper. Or—maybe you'd like to try a piece of aluminum foil. Or a crunched-up piece that's like a ball. What happens to a leaf, a penny, a pencil, or a safety pin?

Aren't sponge animals fun to play with? Don't they seem to get heavier when they're wet?

Did those spoons, corks, or straws sink or float?

What a wonderful canoe that cake of soap makes!

and

THAT BATHBRUSH IS A GREAT OCEAN LINER!

Go for a horseback ride with a hobbyhorse you make all by yourself.
You need a broomstick with a big sock over the end of the broom. (This is the horse's head.)
Then you stuff the head with cloth.
And then just tie the head tight around the end of the broomstick.
NOW GO OFF ON YOUR RIDE!

Find a small spot in your garden that could be your very own.
Then let it be wild.

Let the weeds
grow
and
grow.
Let the wildflowers
flower
and
flower.
The birds will love you, and your spot will be so pretty!

On a fall walk, gather:
dried weeds
leaves
twigs
seed pods
pebbles
nuts
mosses

and when it's cold outside:

Can you make bouquets of the weeds?
Can you look at some of them with your magnifying glass?
You can make a patio for your dollhouse with the pebbles.
If you play with trains, can you use some of the pebbles for boulders that your toy trains pass?
What else can you do with your wonderful fall collection?

Turn over a small patch of soil in your backyard.
You may find some
millipedes
centipedes
sowbugs
ants
worms
and other tiny creatures.
Look at them carefully.
Don't they all seem so busy and work so hard?
Do you ever wonder why? Do you think they may be working to make the soil rich for our garden?

Be a weather forecaster and make a weather chart. Here's how:

Get out a big sheet of paper.
If it's sunny out, use your orange crayon to show the sun.
If it's a rainy day out, make little dots with your black or gray crayon.
If it's cloudy, can you make puffy clouds?
What would you do for a snowy day?
What would you do if it were sunny and then got cloudy?
And if it were cloudy, what would you do if it got sunny?
Would you like to include the moon—a full moon, a half, or a crescent one?

Find one leaf that you like a lot. Besides liking its smell and color, what can you do with this leaf? Can you:

Mount the leaf on a board and hang it up where others in the family will enjoy it too?
Trace the leaf, color it, and cut it out?

Put the leaf on the table and cover it with paper. Then rub back and forth over the leaf with the side of the crayon until the leaf's outlines appear.
Place the leaf between pieces of waxed paper. Then (with a grown-up watching you) press the paper together with a warm iron.

* Any of these ideas would make a very special mobile for the window!

Bend down to enjoy the plant or plants that are growing in just the tiny crack in the sidewalk.

Did you ever find a plant growing in the chink of a wall?

If the plant flowers (as most plants do), smell it.

(Even if it's just one blade of grass—you'll water it if it seems thirsty—won't you?)

Think about all the things a circle can be.

Can a circle be:

a ring?
a balloon?
a snowball?
money?
the top of an ice cream cone?
the sun?
a clown's funny nose?

What about a square?

Can it be a house?
What else?

What about a triangle?

Can it be a teepee?

What are some things a line can be?

Did you ever see a mouse's tail?
or
a piece of thread?

See what you can do with an old sheet.

Can you paint on it?

Can you make a tent between two chairs?

Can you use it for a tablecloth and picnic at the park?

Can you hop on it? Walk on it?

Can you tear it up into a million pieces? (You can also "play doctor" with some of the pieces—can't you?)

Think of how it would be to be

a mischief-making monkey

a splishy, splashy duck
a trumpeting elephant
a fly or a snake
a snail running like a dog
a goat quacking like a duck
an oinking hen
or
a sheep cock-a-doodle-dooing

ABRACADABRA!—
Now you can be all these silly things!

If at all possible, try to go on a train ride—
and
ride past
houses and trees
and
woods
and
rivers
and
telephone lines and poles
and
houses and trees
and
woods
and
rivers
and
telephone lines and poles
and . . .

Everyone pack into the car and go to the fair.
Soar high up in the air on the huge Ferris wheel.
Ride the zooming roller coaster.
Get on the merry-go-round
and
jump on a horse
climb up on an elephant

or

a camel with two humps.

See skeletons in the haunted house

and

Top things off with cotton candy.

DID YOU EVER HAVE SUCH FUN IN YOUR LIFE?

Watch the birds.

Did you know that bird-watching is one of the very few things you can do all year long?

Of course it's easier for children in the spring, when the air is warmer and you can see:

birds flying about with their mates

birds building their babies' nest

AND (if you are very, very lucky)

BIRDS FEEDING THEIR BABIES.

Suppose you were a fish.

Can you swim?

Can you dart away?

Suppose you were a turtle.

Can you crawl?

Can you hide your head and hands under your shell?

What else can you do like a turtle?

Suppose you were a dog.

Can you jump?

Can you crawl under the sofa?

What else can you do like a dog?

Autumn is such a great time of the year—isn't it?

You can watch the leaves dancing on the trees.

Then later, you can watch the leaves floating and tumbling down in the breeze.

Still later, watch how they blow around and then seem to sleep on the ground.

Now—

It's time to get out your rake and rake the leaves from the lawn.

What can you do with the leaves?

If you have a big pile of them, you can jump on them.
You can stomp on them.
You can hide from your friends under them.
THEN—be sure to add your leaves to the compost pile.

Play the "noise" game. It's very simple to play; someone makes a noise, and (without looking) another person guesses what made the noise.

Here are some noises to start out with:
a pencil dropping to the floor
a window being opened and closed
a door being locked or opened and closed
a floor being swept
dishes being washed
a penny being tapped on the window

Take a "listening" walk around the block.

What do you hear?
dogs barking?
birds singing?
lawn mowers whirling?
a radio playing from an open window?
people talking on porches?
the mail carrier chatting with a neighbor?
a mother calling her child to come in for lunch?
acorns falling from the oak trees that line the streets?
windows rattling? (Yes!—windows make sounds too.)
zoom—an airplane that just took off?
the slamming of garbage cans?
Anything else?

Go camping for the night with one of your parents.

Before going into your tent, as it gets dark and quiet—
Take a short walk together.
Doesn't it look like the moon is taking a walk with you?
Do you feel a little night breeze?
Do you hear a frog jump and birds call?
How much fun it is to curl up together under a warm woolly blanket!

Then in the morning, make a small fire together.
Roll up the tent and the blankets
and
Head for home.

Don't you think you both will always remember this time together with love?

Think about how lucky you are to have friends who like you—and always stick by you—no matter what.

Even if you feel very mad about something—your friend won't mind and will still think you're a great pal.

Even if you don't catch on to things fast—your friend will think you're O.K. and will want to help you.

If your skin is a different color—your friend will love you anyway and always stick by you.

If your friend has lots of toys and you have just a few—he won't mind and will be glad to have you come over and play with him—any time!

Make some kind of line on the ground or floor (with chalk or a rope or a piece of string)

and

See how many things you can do with the line.

Can you jump over it?
walk on it?
hop on it?
tiptoe on it?
Can you run around it?

Look out your window.

Isn't it interesting—that every single time we look out the window, we see a different picture? We never seem to see the very same picture twice.

Like:

the sunset
the moon—full, half, or crescent
birds flying by or just one on the grass
snowflakes or rain
stars or no stars
children out playing different games

Go to a pond to watch the ducks.

Watch the ducks—how they always seem to be in pairs
whether they are in the sand
or
in the water.
They almost always seem to be following each other around.
(Do you think they're playing "Follow the Leader"?)
Watch a duck scratch itself with its bill.
(Do you know that bills are also good for scooping up a drink of water?)
Watch how awkwardly a duck waddles on the grass—
and then,
how gracefully the duck glides over the water.
Watch a duck and her ducklings come paddling along.
Wouldn't you love to have them paddle near you?
WAIT! THEY ARE!

Be a sculptor.

The first thing to do is get a bag full of scraps and junk, like:

boxes—big and little
scraps—big and little
jar lids
bottles—plastic bottles (not glass, which can be dangerous when broken)
and

anything else you can find.

Then start gluing the things on top of one another as high as you can. (Glue junk on the sides too.)

You can be sure your masterpiece will be very much admired and (maybe) be placed in the living room!

Some fall afternoon, attend a fall festival fair with the family. What a treat it is for everyone! You can:

Wander through the forests of oaks, willows, and blazing sugar maples.

Go for a hayride.

Try square dancing.

Sip some hot or cold cider.

Learn how to make a wreath.

Make a scarecrow to take home.

Watch someone carving from wood.

Go on a chrysanthemum walk to see thousands and thousands of chrysanthemums blooming.

Paint a pumpkin and join a great pumpkin parade of ghosts and goblins.

Try not to miss the fall festival fair. You'll remember it your whole life!

Wouldn't you love to see a real crane stand for hours and hours on just ONE leg?

And—better yet—

Wouldn't you love to see a real crane dance wildly with BOTH legs in the air?

Why don't you be a crane and see how long you can stand still on just one leg?

How long can you stand on one leg
and
jump up
and
down?

Did you ever think of how much you can learn by just watching "ears"?

Look at your rabbit's ears.
If they're set back to back, the rabbit is on guard, but things are O.K.
If the ears are lifted straight up, the rabbit is really worried
but
When the ears are down—all is well.
IF one ear is bent forward and the other ear is bent backward, the rabbit is thinking:
"Now just where did that noise come from?"

Play "Charades."
(You don't know how to play "Charades"?) In "Charades" you act out a word
a sentence
the title of a book
a song
or even a famous person (like the president!)
Then, the job of the others is to guess who or what you're acting out. This game is really tons of fun!

Go for a hat hunt around the house and make a hat store.
Collect whatever hats you can find:
swim hats
sun hats
straw hats
fur hats
firefighter hats if your mother or father is a firefighter
a police officer's hat
a hard hat for a construction worker
a miner's hat with a lamp
a bicycle helmet
Do you have a baby's bonnet?
Be sure to have a mirror in your store so hats can be tried on before they are bought.
Also, be sure all the hats are put back where they came from when you close your store.

Try some of these "Who Am I's" with a friend.
Here's one to begin with.
"My fur is brown.
I make chipping sounds.
I love nuts and hide them to eat later.
What animal am I?" (a chipmunk)
Now make up your own.

Try to attend a program of the touring National Theater of the Deaf.
You'll be surprised how much you understand even if the actors don't say a single word out loud.

Watch a big fat frog wait to catch a worm.

Ask someone to help you change the furniture of your room around.
Isn't it great to give your room a "new look"?

Think about this:
Do you know that without plants there would be no animals—and you wouldn't be here, and nobody you know would be here either?
We all need plants:
to grow
to move around
and
to think.
Everything fits together.

What plants do you eat?
lettuce?
broccoli?
spinach?
bread (made from wheat or other plants)?

What else?
What plants do we use for building houses
and
tables and chairs?

Are plants used to help people when they get sick?

AREN'T YOU GLAD WE HAVE PLANTS?

Make a tiger mask from a brown bag and crawl about scaring everyone in the house.
Grr Grr Grr

Just listen to the bluebird singing in the apple tree.

Snuggle up in bed with your little sister.
Do you feel like two little bugs in a rug?

Get together a pile of "moving" words.
Then someone act out the word and someone else guess what the "moving" word is:
Here are some:
stretching
tiptoeing
twirling
wobbling
dancing
wiggling
bouncing
shivering
wiggling
running
walking
jumping
bowling
swaying

stumbling
leaping
spinning

Try snoozing and sneezing. They don't move a lot—but they still move!

Try to get hold of an old-fashioned wood clothespin so you can make a clothespin doll.

If you want a dress for your doll, just wrap bits of cloth around the clothespin.

If you want pants for your doll, wrap bits of cloth around the two prongs.

If you need a belt—a piece of ribbon will be just right.

If you want hair for your doll—do you have some yarn you can use?

If you need arms, then a straw is good or else a pipe cleaner.

For the head, get out your crayons or a ballpoint pen—and put in the eyes, mouth, and the nose.

Now you have your clothespin doll!

If you have many old-fashioned clothespins, you can line them up along the edge of a pan.

Talk about YOU.

Can you answer:

My name is________________________.
I live at__________________________.
My friends are______________________.
I am happiest when__________________.
My mother is________________________.
My father is________________________.
My favorite things are______________.
I just love_________________________.
I get angry when____________________.

I like stories that_______________.
When I was little, I_______________.
I feel proud when_________________.
I wish someone would help me_______.
I look forward to_________________.
I don't understand why_____________.
If I had three wishes, I___________.
Someday I would like to____________.

Look out from your window and see the downtown skyscraper.
Doesn't it look just like it's scraping the sky?
(No wonder it's called "skyscraper"!)

Play tiddledywinks with your best friend.
Wouldn't it be great if you could play as long as you wanted to without having to yell out:
"But Mom—we just started to have fun!"

Tuck all your dolls in bed.
Can you make up a "good-night" story for them?

Stuff an old nylon stocking to make a big, soft toy for the baby to play with.

Get out a pencil and a piece of paper and just play around with lines.

See if you can make squiggly, straight, fat, or thin lines.

Can you make lines that are fuzzy, go around in circles, and look like dust storms?

What about lines that are very sharp and go straight up and down?

Lines can really give ideas like action, joy, or tiredness.

They really can!

Do you know that lines can be mountains?

Lines can be trees. Lines can even give you an idea that trees are far away. How would you draw a line to represent a faraway tree?

Help your brother rake the leaves.

Then
sit down and play checkers
or
flop down on the grass and rest
from all your hard work.

Play with your Erector set.

If you build a palace,
the sofa can be the mountains near the palace
and
the rug can be the nearby sea.

Try to rub your tummy and pat your head at the same time. It isn't easy, but try it anyway.

Watch a litter of puppies at play.

Aren't they such fun to watch?

Make shadow pictures. It's so easy and so much fun. You can make a scrapbook with shadow pictures of all your friends.

Here's all you do:

Tack a sheet of white paper on the wall.

Have a friend sit in front of the paper. The shadow of his head should fall on the paper when you shine a flashlight on him.

Draw a pencil line around the shadow.

Take the paper off the wall and cut along the line.

Glue the shadow picture on black paper so that it stands out clearly.

And that's all.

Scout around for unwanted *National Geographic* magazines. They are a perfect place to find pictures of faraway lands for making collages and books to show:

how people faraway live
how they dress
what they look like
their homes
the work they do
the foods they eat
their dances
the toys they have
their birds, trees, flowers, and animals
Some even carry their babies in different ways.

AREN'T DIFFERENCES BEAUTIFUL?

Tie a string to your wrist and attach a balloon to the other end.
If the string isn't too long, see if you can bounce it on the floor.
If the string is a long one, will the balloon hit the ceiling?

What do you think of when you hear the word "porcupine"—do you think mostly of prickles?
What about a skunk—its smell?
Is a bear mostly gr-rrrr?
What about a bee? Bzzzzzz?
Do you think of a huge mouth when you think of a crocodile?
What about a leopard? spots?
owls? hoots?
a duck? quacks?

a zebra? stripes?

What about a camel? its humps? Would you like to take a ride between them?

Just stop to think a bit—

that long ago there weren't any cars

no trains

no trucks

no airplanes

Does it make you wonder how people ever managed?

Make believe you're dancing with a scarecrow.

(Scarecrows know how to dance. They really do!)

Make a crown of braided daisies, dandelions, or other pretty flowers.

(You might like it even more than a crown of gold or silver!)

If it's a boiling hot summer day, find a big leaf from a maple tree and fan yourself with it.

Watch a tumbleweed tumble along

as it takes its baby seeds for a

long ride in the wind.

Go to some of these places if you can.

Local newspapers are a gold mine of great things you and the family can enjoy.

a sidewalk art show

the opening of a new public building

a cherry orchard that's in full bloom

a street fair that's selling used books

a soapbox derby contest

an outdoor poetry reading

a free film at the library

Is there a band concert at the park or at the public square?
How would you like to hear a concert UNDER THE STARS?

Start a collection of different kinds and colors of bird feathers.
What a great feather scrapbook it would make
or
What a fine display it could make for the family bulletin board.
Keep your eyes open for
pigeon feathers
goose feathers
duck feathers
chicken feathers
There may be a feather in your home right this minute, a feather from your pet canary!

Draw five things you like to eat.
Now draw five things you don't like to eat.
(Do you think these would be good hints for your mother?)

Try a treat you'll never forget—
Eat a warm tomato you picked right from the garden.

Look at the biggest trees on your block.
Can you find one whose roots have pushed the sidewalk up?
Be careful—don't trip.

Make a humming flute.
Punch three or four holes in the side of a cardboard tube (like a paper-towel tube or a toilet-tissue tube).
Cover one end with a piece of waxed paper, held in place with a rubberband
and
Hum into the other end, moving your fingers over the holes.
(It's just like playing a real flute!)

Go out to eat with the family. Have you ever visited a restaurant that serves only foreign foods, like:

sukiyaki?
tacos?
Wienerschnitzel?
spaghetti and meatballs?
chop suey?
corned beef and cabbage?
lasagna?
ravioli?
latkes?
pizza?
borschts?

Have a rip-roaring time
and
make a collage of papers torn from:
old greeting cards
crepe paper
wrapping paper
old wallpaper books
napkins
magazines
etc.
Then hang it up with clothespins on a rope between two chairs for your admirers.

Just watch your pet turtle swim in the water.
See how it glides using its legs like flippers.

Search for hiding places of insects.
Look under rocks and stones
along fences
old boards
a bunch of old decayed leaves and grass.
Do you have a hiding place too?

Do you like a hiding place where you can be by yourself with no one to disturb you?
That's probably the way insects feel.
That's probably why it's always a good idea to
take a peek
and then
put back the rocks, leaves, twigs, etc.—right where you found them.

Have fun drawing make-believe footprints of:
an elephant
a hippopotamus
a giraffe
and
a person.

Get out your blocks and building toys and build castles, palaces, and big mountains.

Sit in the backyard in the warm, early-autumn sun and grow very lazy.

Listen to the spring peepers in the woods.
What do you think they're saying to one another?

Curl up under a blanket with your treasured teddy bear and make up a "going-to-bed" song or poem for it.

Pretend you are walking in a jungle
or
crossing a desert
or
undertaking a mountain climbing expedition.

* Bring a few friends on your journey.

Visit the bakery shop.

Wouldn't it be great if the owner would let you watch the bakers at work!

Yummy—chocolate brownies
lemon tarts
all kinds of doughnuts
(Don't you wish you could buy them all for ten cents?)

Look for moss on the bark of a tree.

Now look for moss on another tree.
And another.

Is the moss always on the sunny or the shady side of the tree? Why do you think this is so?

Go barefoot in your house and feel each floor with your feet.

How does the tile in the bathroom feel?
How does the living room floor feel? the kitchen?
What about the concrete in the basement?

Get hold of a big box.

Get into it.
Pretend you are a jumping jack
and
jump out of it.

Spread out a tablecloth on the dining room floor

or
beside a fireplace
and have an indoor picnic.

Try some of these nuts:

walnuts (wonderful in muffins)
almonds (add to stir-fry)
coconuts (just right for the tops of cupcakes or birthday cakes)
peanuts (for making peanut butter for a delicious peanut butter sandwich!)
pecans (DID YOU EVER TASTE A PECAN PIE?)

Think about things that change.
A seed can become a tree.
What can come from a grape?
Where does cider come from?
What can a baby become?

Just think of how much fun it would be to have a porcupine as a pet, or
a gorilla
or
perhaps a rhinoceros.
You could go on a nice walk in the park or just play together.

Collect old pieces of yarn, ribbon, straw, and such things.
In the spring, put the collection outdoors where birds will see it.
Wait till a bird discovers the collection and don't be surprised at how fast everything disappears!
(You know what for—don't you?)

Before you go fishing with your big brother, help dig up some worms.
(Even if you don't catch any fish—isn't it fun anyway?)

Make a list of things you like a lot, things like:
cats

kites
picnics
mud pies
chocolate chip cookies.
What else?

Be a "discoverer."
All you have to do is stake your claim by circling a rope on the ground anywhere you like.
Then look carefully at everything inside your circle—animals, plants, rocks, and shells.
How many things can you discover?
(You don't have to know their names.)

Someday when you're at a farm, watch a mother pig giving birth to piglets in her sty.
Isn't it interesting to see?
And can you watch the mother pig nursing her babies—wouldn't that be a double treat?

If you can possibly get to the wharf of your city—
Sit as long as you can
and
Watch ships from distant lands coming and going.

See if there are any gulls in the parking lot of the shopping plaza.
Isn't it fun to see them strutting around?

Make an outline of your friend.
All you have to do is:
Have your friend lie down on a big piece of paper.
Draw an outline of your friend's body.
Color in everything you want to.
Roll up the paper when you're done.
Tie it with a string.

And then
Give it to your friend.
(She may want to give it to her mother or grandparents as a present.)

Find a pretty little buttercup and look at it very closely.
Smell it. Now look in the mirror.
What's that yellow stuff on your nose?
Look at it carefully. Doesn't it really look like a cup with some butter in it?
After a while, put the little buttercup in a cup filled with water for when it gets thirsty.
Then set it on the middle of the breakfast table for everyone to enjoy.

Watch the two strong grown-ups picking up the neighbor's furniture and carrying it to the big moving van.
Don't they make it look easy?
Do you think it is?

Think of what a frog would sound like if it purred like a cat. Think of what a dog would sound like if it roared like a lion.
Suppose a duck mooed like a cow.
How would you like sounding like a buzzing bee?

Just think about this . . .
If someone ever wanted to hurt you, what would you do to protect yourself?
Suppose you were a lion, would you roar?
What would a dog do? (Did you ever see a dog's teeth?)
Why do you think a deer has horns?
Just about everyone knows what a porcupine would do. Do you?

Make a fairyland of shapes by
patting
poking

piling
and
smoothing moist sand.
Can you also build roads that lead to mountains
and
Can you build a road tunnel into the mountain?

Sit on the floor with your friend and pull each other back and forth like a rowing machine. When you do this, sing:

"Row, row, row your boat
Gently down the stream.
Merrily, merrily, merrily, merrily,
Life is but a dream."

Start a collection of nature posters that are usually put out by travel agencies.

For example:
posters of Niagara Falls
posters of the Grand Canyon

Once you start a collection of nature posters, you will learn a lot about our big, beautiful country.

* Nature postcards are fun to collect too.

Get out the oldest photo album that you have.
Do you see pictures of your grandmother when she was little?
How did she look? Was she pretty? What were her clothes like? Are there pictures of her mother or father holding her?
What was her house like?
When your grandmother looks at these pictures, too, does she have a kind of special look on her face?

Think of all the things you have that come in pairs,
things like:
mittens
boots
shoes

house slippers.
Don't forget earmuffs
and
roller skates!
What else?

Try this experiment.
Do you want to see how the tubes of a stalk of celery absorb water?
Just cut off the bottom of a celery stalk.
Place the rest of the stalk in a glass of colored water.
(You can color it with beet juice or food coloring.)
Wait about an hour
And see what happens.

On a windy spring day—
Watch a cherry or an
apple tree
and
chase after the cherry
blossoms when they fall
like snowflakes.

When you go shopping—bring along a bunch of used paper bags.
You'll be helping the family
and
You'll be helping to save trees!

Make a snowman on your front lawn so he or she can invite company in.
Be sure the snowman has an old pipe to smoke
an old hat to wear
a scarf to keep warm
and
some coal (or buttons if you don't have coal)
for eyes
nose

and
grin!

On a lazy afternoon
when you and your father don't feel like doing anything special—
sit out on the porch steps
look into the deep blue sky
and
watch the fluffy white clouds change from one shape to another.

If you live near a Native American Reservation—
attend the yearly summer festival.
You'll love the dancing and the songs.
Also, they will probably be wearing beautiful clothing much like what their parents and their parents' parents wore a long time ago.

Listen to the whistle of the train as it goes far off down the track—far into the night.

Place a pan of water in the sun and
another pan of water in a dark place.
Check them each day to see what happens.

Don't let anyone know where you are.
Crawl under the clothes basket.
Poke out your head.
Walk around the room.
And everyone will think there's a turtle in the house. They really will!

Try to juggle one or two balls at one time.
It isn't easy, but try anyway.

Listen to stories where everything seems as if it's so near, but is really far, far away.
Stories about:
animals prowling in jungles
sailing the oceans
going to the moon
or
panthers prowling
beneath banana trees.

See if you can stand upside down.

Make up a bowling game—use old tin cans to knock over with a ball.

Make a chain that will reach all the way to the moon.
All you need to do is cut out skinny strips of paper, fold each strip into a loop, and
paste the ends of each loop together, looping each loop through the loop you just made.
Do this: again
and
again
and
again . . .
Would you like to make a chain of different colors to decorate your bedroom?

Sail a boat on the green ocean of your lawn.
For this great adventure you need:
a box

a stick
a string for fishing equipment
two sticks for oars
and
another stick to raise a piece of cloth for a flag.
Then sail away!

Look as closely as you can at the beak of a bird on the grass. Is it strong and pointed? It's just right for getting grubs and other insects from the lawn.

Pretend you are a rubber ball
and
bounce
and
bounce
and
bounce.

See if you can balance a
ball on your nose and
then let it roll down on your chest.

Enjoy a walk in the forest—but a different kind of walk.
Enjoy a walk when it is so quiet, you can almost
hear an insect boring a tunnel inside a log.
Sh Sh
or
hear the whispering sounds of a growing fern pushing aside dead leaves.
And
You can hear the ferns unrolling their fiddle-shaped heads, their heads slowly, slowly stretching upward.
Sh Sh Sh

Watch the birds flying in the sky.
Do you know that some birds fly thousands of miles, then come back to the very same special spot to lay their eggs?
(Birds are very smart, aren't they?)

Play with your jack-in-the-box.
BUT be sure it doesn't bop you right in the nose!

Draw a picture of the tree in the front of your house.
If you draw a picture of it in the spring, in the summer, the fall, and the winter—you will see how it changes and how beautiful it is every season.

Strum on the worn strings of the old banjo that nobody plays anymore.

Figure out all the things you can do with a scarf:
With a scarf around you, you can be:
a butterfly
a dancing wave
a fairy
or
an eagle in the sky.

Listen to the birds.
Listen to the birds in the morning.
Do they sound different from how they sound at night?
Did you ever hear a bird call—
and
another bird answer?

Make somersaults on the living room carpet.
If the space is clear,
can you make somersaults from one end to the other?

In the spring,
search for treasures hidden for months and months under the ice and snow.
(Did you find any pennies or a big quarter?)

Spy on a spider!
Try to find a spider that's just beginning to spin a web.
Have you ever watched a spider repair a web?
Did you ever see a spider pounce on an insect?

Play a game of "basketball" by sailing playing cards into a box.

When your parents go on their next trip to buy groceries, go to the produce department.
Don't the fruits and vegetables look like a beautiful bouquet of flowers?
What do you see that's red? (apples? beets? strawberries?)
What do you see that's orange? (oranges? carrots?)
Is there anything green? (lettuce? green peppers?)
What about brown? (potatoes?)
Is there anything purple? (grapes? purple cabbage?)
See how some things are:
little and round
long and thin
hard or soft.
Some things are hard outside and soft inside.
How many of these will you eat today that will make you strong and healthy and are so DELICIOUS too?

Find several of your friends to see who can make the biggest pile of spring words in ten minutes.
Here are a few to start you off:
butterflies

seeds
robins
running brooks
lilacs
daffodils

Try the same thing with summer words.
Here are a few summer words:
ice-cream cones
swimming
marigolds
hiking
roller skating

Now try fall and winter. Next, the holidays, such as Christmas.

Listen to this loving poem by Malaika Hart.
Listen to it over and over again.
You can almost sing it—can't you?

Ants
Crawl around,
They have a sound.
Who hears the sound?
Me, the morning star.

Bunnies and rabbits have a little sound,
They hop on the ground.
They hop all around.

In the bushes
There are little things looking at you
They have very big eyes.
Rabbits.

The spider web
Looks like the masts
Of a pirate ship

Help make a compost pile for your garden.
Here's all that needs to be done:
Make a hole or use a large bucket.

Add banana peels
left-overs from making a salad
apple cores
grass
autumn leaves
and
a few cups of soil.
Then, turn over the contents every few weeks.
The worms and other tiny animals will have a delicious treat as they turn your compost pile into beautiful, wonderful, rich soil!

Look at the colors around you.
Look for colors of cars
houses
animals
insects
books
toys
the clothes people wear
Did you ever see the colors of a rainbow? a sunset?

Figure this out.
What is the difference between a "living" thing and something that isn't a "living" thing?
For example:
Is a dog a living thing?
Is a toy dog a living thing?
Is an airplane a living thing?
Is a bird a living thing?
Is a picture of a bird a living thing?
Is a flower a living thing?
You're right! All living things can make more living things. Isn't that interesting?
Now go for a walk and look for living things and some things that are non-living.

Walk down the street just to look at the lovely bushes growing in front of your neighbors' houses.

Enjoy their colors, their smells, their flowers, and their different-shaped leaves.
What's that shining beneath that bush? IT'S A NICKEL!

Set up a centerpiece for the table.
It doesn't always have to be of flowers—
why not a bunch of autumn leaves?
a pumpkin? or a squash?
some pinecones?
a basket of washed stones or rocks?
If your fish tank isn't too large, why not set that in the center?
Centerpieces don't always have to be there just because they're pretty to look at; they can also be lots of fun to talk about and learn from.

Poke holes in dirt or sand with a stick.
What animals can you find?
What are they doing?
Follow them for a while.
Can you make up a story pretending you are an animal living there?

Listen to the key turning in the lock.
Can you guess who's coming home?
Is it your mother coming home from work?
Are you ready for your hugs and kisses?

Get your big brother or sister to give you a piggy-back ride to your bed.
Isn't it fun?

Did you ever wonder what the children one thousand years from now will be like?

Look up and watch a pair of robins building their nest in a tree.
Can you see the blue eggs the mother laid?
Can you see the little babies come out after the eggs crack?
(Maybe say something nice to them, but don't touch them.)
Isn't it fun to see how the mother and father go back and forth bringing the babies bugs and worms to eat?
Soon they will learn to fly and will fly away on their own.
Do you know that someday they will be mommies and daddies too?

Think of things that *you* like that other people *may not* like.
For example:
Do you like to pick up worms and watch them wiggle?
Lots of people wouldn't think of picking up a worm.
Isn't it fun to play in dirt?
Lots of people wouldn't think of playing in dirt.
Do you enjoy looking for rocks and stones?
Some people don't care about stones at all.
What other things can you think of that you like and others don't?
YOU ARE SPECIAL!

Smell the smell of a
bakery
beauty salon
Laundromat
pet shop
and (oh yes!)
a flower shop.
Don't they all seem to have their own special smell?
Even sheets that are hung out to dry on the line have their own special smell—don't they?

Tap on the floor and make sounds that are soft
like a pussy cat purring
like rain falling.
Can you make the sound of a wild thunderstorm?

Make a collection of things in your house made of rubber.
Can you find:
a rubber band?
a balloon?
a rubber ball?
an eraser?
elastic on your underpants?
What else?
Another day you may want to make a collection of things made from:
metal
wood
cloth
or
plastic

Do you know that you can make a "bridge" with a board?
All you need besides a board is a pile of old telephone books to support each end of it.
(Be careful—don't fall in the water!)

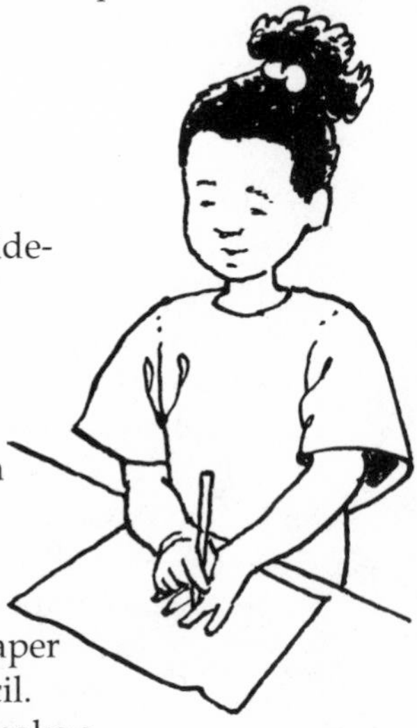

Make a bath for the birds. It's easy.
All you have to do is fill a dishpan (or an upside-down garbage can lid) with water
and
place it outdoors.
But
you have to be absolutely sure you put it high enough so that cats can't get at it easily!

Put your hand down flat on a piece of paper
and follow the shape of it with a pencil.
If you cut out the shape with scissors, it will make a gift any grandparent in the world would treasure.
(Also important is to put the date on it or have someone do it for you.)

If you live in the country and come into the city—
wouldn't it be fun just to go window-shopping?

If you don't know how to write yet—
Tell a story to a grown-up
and ask the grown-up to write it down on a big piece of paper.
Then all you have to do is make pictures for it.
(An old wallpaper sample will make a great cover.)
Then share your book with a friend.

Go visit your neighbor who practices the piano, guitar, flute, or trumpet every day.
Do you know someone who loves to sing and you could go hear him or her practice?
When you go to hear them, doesn't it seem as if you have your own private concert?

When it's too hot for sleeping indoors,
camp out in your backyard with your sleeping bag.
(Of course, you can only do this if your parents know it is safe.)

Get out your blackboard and chalk and draw what you see when you look out the window.
Do you see:
a bird on a post?
an old man taking a walk with his dog?
a delivery truck?
a cat?
a mouse scampering from your house to the neighbor's house?

Listen to the birds chirping in the morning outside your window.
Isn't it one of the sweetest sounds you've ever heard?

Listen to the church bells chiming.
What song do you hear?
What time is it?

Listen carefully to words people use when they talk to you.
Have you ever noticed how people will do lots of things for you if you use words like:
please?
and
thank you?
Maybe that's why they're called "magic words."
Can you think of any other words that are called polite words or magic words?

Play "Little Sir Echo."
You be "Little Sir Echo." Someone else says anything—perhaps like "How are you today?" Then you must say the same thing—a lot more quietly.
It's lots of fun. Try it!

Enjoy the magic of picking up a bunch of pins with a magnet.
What else can you pick up with a magnet?
Will it pick up pens?
pencils?
paper clips?
erasers?
paper?
staples?
a penny?
another magnet?
Try out some other things about the house and yard.

Draw pictures on the sides of a brown paper bag.
If you draw a picture of a face,

stuff the bag with old paper,
and close off the top,
this could be your friend when you get lonely sometime.

If you're lucky enough to live near the ocean—
or
even just able to visit the ocean—
look at the powerful waves that
curl
billow and roar
slap and splash
flap and flop
and
foam
rush
and
roar
and
rise so high!

Doesn't the ocean have a kind of endless look about it?
Try to spend enough time to see the tide come in and go out. You'll never forget it!

Look carefully at the pinecone you brought home from your walk.
Do you know that this pinecone is like a nursery for seeds?
(Seeds stay in the nursery until they fall to the ground.)
Do you know what happens then? They become giant pine trees.
(It is strongly suggested that you find the seeds before those squirrels get them and eat them for lunch!)

Find a secret place—maybe an overturned chair in the backyard
or
maybe a huge umbrella.
Be a real lazy bones and dream
of

Pinocchio
The Pied Piper of Hamelin
or
Alice's Adventures in Wonderland.

Take your dog for a walk in the morning.
What about taking your dog for a walk after dinner too?
(Your parents who have been working all day would really appreciate it.)

Check out the house to see if there are any lights, radios, TV sets, or computers on—but not being used.
Can you turn them off by yourself or get someone older to do it for you?

Visit the woods; you can learn so many things you'll never learn anywhere else:
about frog orchestras
about the family of bugs on the dead log
about the many textures of tree bark
the soft beds of mosses
the holes small forest animals make to live in
Do try to visit the woods as often as you can.
There's so much to learn about—wonderful things just waiting for you!

How would you like a new friend?
Why not adopt a nearby tree
and
Keep a box or scrapbook of its:
leaves
buds
seeds
flowers
bits of bark
and
drawings you make of it from season to season.

Find an old rubber tire
and
roll it up and down your block.
Can you roll it with a stick or is it easier with just your hand?

Bring along a small bag of fat crayons and some paper when you go for a long, boring wait at a doctor's or a dentist's office.

If it's boiling hot outside—
Cool off when the city opens up the fire hydrant and floods your street.

Listen to the birds sing. Have you ever wondered why birds sing?
Do they sing to let another bird know when there is danger around and to be careful?
Do they sing to let other birds know there is food around?
Are birds singing because they want to mate?

Look at all the pine trees, each in front of the houses across the street where you live.
Don't they look like a lot of giant hairbrushes?

Take a walk in the deep snow with your mother.
If you walk behind her, you'll be able to walk in her boot prints. (You may have to hold on to her coat too!)

Find out how old your sister is and draw a tree or a flower for each year of her life.
Can you do the same thing for your best friend?
Can you do it for "you"?

Build a skyscraper with boxes.
Keep going. You can build a box town too!

Give your mother a kiss and a hug—one for every day of the week.
That's seven kisses and hugs all at one time!

Check out your gerbil cage to see what's going on there.
Aren't you glad you have gerbils for pets?
Aren't gerbils the cutest, most curious little characters you ever saw?
Gerbils are very clean, always washing their hands and rubbing their fur. And, if you look at their tongues, you'll see that they are rough like cats', who spend so much time cleaning themselves.
Also, gerbils are easy to feed. A day's feeding is just a few tablespoons of dry birdseed and a bit of lettuce or fruit. And they also need some water.

In the summer, when the water is warmed by the sun—
Take an outdoor shower with your hose.
With your soap
and
towel
and
fluffy bathrobe.
And when you hear the birds and feel a gentle wind—isn't this a kind of Garden of Eden?

Build a tunnel with your blocks—
and build it so trains can go through.

Get out your "follow the dots" book and do a few pages.

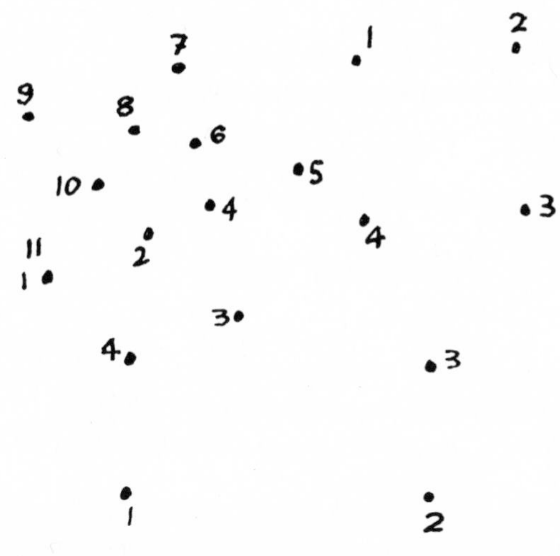

Play Leap Frog with your friends.
Can you jump over your friends' shoulders?

Eat a box of Cracker Jack—and, if you find a paper whistle inside or something you always wanted—
wouldn't that MAKE YOUR DAY?

Make a wildflower notebook with the pressed flowers you found on your hiking trip.
What a marvelous collection you can have as you get older and older, adding new ones after each hike.
Will you have pearly everlasting?
bleeding heart?
jack-in-the-pulpit?
If you are lucky enough to find a Jack, lift up his hood and you will know how he got his name. He looks just like he's preaching a sermon to the robins and squirrels—and sometimes, even to the chipmunks!

Collect old unwanted newspapers,
wallpaper, wrapping paper, tissue paper

and any other paper you can find.
Tear them up into big and little pieces
and then
arrange the pieces into pictures.
Paste them down
and
You'll have a collage anyone would really enjoy!

Mow the lawn.

When you see "weeds" in the lawn—don't pull them out.

Most weeds have pretty flowers. And besides, some weeds (like chickweed) are great for birds to eat. Yes!

Go coasting on your brand new red sled.

Is your sled big enough for you and a friend so that you can go coasting together?

After grocery shopping with Mom or Dad

Can you stop off for a treat—maybe an ice cream cone or a hot chocolate?

Whenever you can—

Touch a rose petal. How does it feel?

Hold a new little puppy. Do you like the way she feels?

Did you feel cold when you went outside? Did you feel better when you buttoned your coat?

When you went fishing, how did it feel when your shoes got wet?

Do you like the feel of the smooth ice when you go ice-skating?

Do you like the feel of your mother's skin?

How does your new little baby sister feel?

Climb on the monkey bars at the park.

(But be careful because monkeys have long tails to hang on with and you DON'T!)

Look at your house and the people who live in it.
Aren't you glad you have all this?
(Many people don't, you know.)

Watch the insect that is swimming so hard to get out of a tiny whirlpool of water.
After a little while, wouldn't you like to help the insect get out and go home?

Watch a nuthatch walking upside down on your tree.
Such an acrobatic bird!
The little nuthatch could be in a circus if it were a person.
Don't you think so?

Stop and think of all the different parts of a plant we eat.
If we eat spinach and lettuce, we eat the leaves of a plant.
When we eat carrots, potatoes, or beets, we eat the roots.
Most of us eat celery. That's the stem of the plant.
Every time we eat peas or beans, we are eating a plant's seeds.
See if you can tell what we eat when we eat cauliflower. (The name itself is a hint on this one!)

See if you can take hold of a teasel plant without being pricked by its large spines.
(Those spines are like a suit of armor to protect the plant!)
If you can, break off a piece or two of the spiny skeleton stalk—and bring it home to put in a jar to admire.

Make a "circle" picture by:
cutting out circles of colored gummed paper
and
sticking them on paper.
It's so easy to do and also lots of fun. See what a grown person comes up with!

When you walk down a long road, doesn't it appear, when it runs far away from you, to get

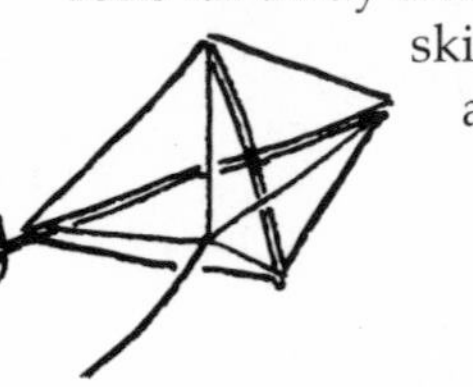

skinnier
and
skinnier
and
skinnier?

Get out of your stuffy house and enjoy the air outdoors.
When you stop to think about it, air is pretty wonderful—isn't it?
Birds can fly in the air.
Leaves and seeds would have nothing to blow about in if there were no air.
Swings would be no use to children if you couldn't swing high in the air.
Do you think a sailboat could sail without air to blow the sails?
What about kites? You MUST have air for the kites to go up high.
Bubble pipes need air too, don't they?
Did the family car or your bicycle ever have a flat tire? They need air for their tires, don't they?
Without airplanes flying in the air, would you be able to visit your grandmother who lives hundreds of miles away?

Play "Kick the Can."
To play "Kick the Can," you just kick a can and see how far it will go.
You can also play this game with a friend and see who can kick it the farthest.

Sniff your way around your block.
What sniffs did you sniff?
a magnolia tree?
tulips?
gasoline?
dead leaves?
newly cut grass?

smoke from a chimney?
a wet dog?
dirty water?
What else?

Carve a beautiful piece of sculpture from a bar of soap with a fingernail file.

* Don't throw away the scraps, because the pieces can be wetted together to make another small bar of soap.

Help make the birthday punch by adding some molasses.

(When you handle the molasses—doesn't the molasses, the way it moves—give you the funniest feeling that it's dragging you down too? Doesn't it, just a little bit?)

Remove the outer skin of a soaked lima bean,
split the bean in half,
and
look at it with a magnifying glass.
Do you see a baby lima bean plant all curled up inside?

Look for animal homes.
Can you find a home for:
a squirrel—a big, heavy nest in a tree?
a dog—a dog house?
a worm—the soil?
What other animal homes can you find?

When you get up in the morning, look out the window to check whether the leaves and branches are moving.

And see if stray papers are skidding all over the pavement.

Do you think you may get an idea of whether it's going to be a windy day or not?

On a summer's day—
Look out at the bees and butterflies sticking their heads into garden blossoms.
Doesn't it seem that insects and flowering plants are made for each other?

If you live near a park—
look out your window when it's dark.
Do you see how the park lights shine—
don't they look like dandelions?

Play with your blocks.
While you play, you can learn lots of things, like:
The taller your skyscraper gets, the easier it can fall.
You can learn some things about building bridges or a levee that would keep rivers from overflowing.
(Pretend you are an engineer and the river is rising.)
Do all blocks have the same weight?
You can learn that round blocks roll and square ones don't
and (this is very important)
you can learn that the more careful you are about building, the more careful the blocks are put on top of one another—the steadier the building will be!

Listen to the cuckoo cooing.
The cuckoo leads such a very busy life searching for flies—so when you do hear a cuckoo singing, be sure to listen.

Gently put the palm of your hand on your throat.
How does it feel
when you talk?
when you sing?
when you hum?

when you blow?
when you SHOUT?

Make believe you have a crocodile in your bathtub.
Wouldn't that be something?
Do you think this crocodile would hurt you?
No—it wouldn't!

In the spring,
when you walk under a tree
and
find egg shells—
listen for baby birds chirping for food.

Invite some people on your block to come to your backyard some evening to
have roast corn
play cards
tell jokes
or
just talk.

Write a letter about pollution to your mayor.
If you don't know how to write yet, your drawings and a few words from a grown-up would be enough.

Think of five sounds that letters of the alphabet make. Now think of a word these letters start. For example:
mmmmmmmm m (man)
OOOOOOOO o (open)
ttttttt t (tree)
Now think of others yourself.

Toss a hoop in the air and see if you can catch it.
How long can you keep the hoop rolling?
Can you jump over a hoop as if you were jumping rope?

Take a ride on your tricycle or your bicycle.
(Can you make it to the top of a steep hill without walking it?)

Go outdoors and—if you look very hard at fallen leaves—you may find a leaf that was almost all eaten by insects.
Look closely. You may be able to see how an insect works.

Cut out the numbers of an old calendar
and make a clock from a paper plate.
If you need help, look at a real clock to copy.

Can you lay out a nature trail around your house or around your block?
If someone new is visiting you, wouldn't it be fun to take the person on your nature trail?

See what a real treat it is to visit the state game farm when hundreds and hundreds of pheasants are released.
Do you wonder where they are going? Would you like to be able to go with them?

Visit a large dam—
one that is used to make electricity
one that makes a lake for swimming
or
one that gives out water when farmers need it to grow their crops.

Play a game called "Running Broad Grin."
It's easy to play and lots of fun because all you have to do is see who can make the broadest, biggest grin.
And that person is the winner!

Play with your stuffed toys.
Do you have stuffed animals like bears and monkeys?
Why not have a tea party for them?

Watch the storage and moving truck pulling up to the house across the street to unload the new owner's belongings.
How would you be able to tell if a new playmate will be coming there to live?

Sing your name.
Can you sing the name of everyone in the family?
Can you sing your address?
and your birthday?

When you're strolling in the park with your dad, stop and listen to an old man playing his guitar.
How can you tell he really loves his guitar?

Ask a grown-up to tie a rope from a high branch of a tree so you can swing on it.
Hold on tight and make believe you're riding on an airplane.

Rummage through your attic.
Is that an old mandolin that your dad played years ago?
Bring it downstairs and get him to play it for you. (He will, if you ask hard enough!)

If there is a slow drip from the bathroom faucet, report it to an adult for repair.
Do you know that a slow drip from a faucet wastes fifty gallons of water in a month?

Think about this—
Some birds like to eat insects.
Some like the nectar of flowers.
and
Some like mice! Yes!

Sample the sweetness that can be sucked from a clover blossom.
Could you tell what it was if your eyes were closed?
If your eyes were closed, and if someone offered you a dandelion green, would you know what it was?

Drop some drops of paint on some paper and blow on the drops through a straw.
Watch the paint "grow" and move around.
(If you use two straws it is even more exciting!)

Listen to a baby breathing.
Listen to a grown-up breathing.
Did you ever hear yourself breathe?
Does your breathing sound the same when you have a cold?

Play a game you can play with two empty spools.
Roll one spool and then watch to see where it stops.
Now roll another spool in the same direction and see if you can make it catch up to the first spool.

*If you play with a friend, see who can roll the spools the farthest.

Go out to smell the perfume of the spring flowers
with their ten thousand colors of blue
and
ten thousand colors of red
and let the wind bathe your face.

While you're helping to shuck the peas—look for a tiny root coming from one of them.
(Do you know that you can shoot a pea out of a straw—but don't ever shoot it on people!)

Try to get hold of a bit of the cookie dough your mother is using
and
make your own cookies.
You can roll it
flatten it
and
cut the cookies into your own shapes or use cookie cutters.
Then have them popped into the oven along with your mother's.
Do you think someone would rather have one of your cookies than one of your mother's?

Plant a tree on Arbor Day, especially if it's a tree you started yourself from a seed you found.
Every year it will grow and grow.
Someday when you are grown up, maybe you'll read a book in the shade of your tree.

Listen to your mother talk to you about things.
Look at her face when she talks. Do you see that she looks right at you and her eyes seem to say, "You're somebody"?
When others talk, see if their eyes look right at you.

Open the refrigerator and get out a piece of celery to munch on.
Celery is noisy—but they say it's healthful
and
it's also good for making your jaws strong.

Keep your eyes open for things in nature that are sort of strange, like:

a tree that's twisted
funny lumps and bumps in leaves
or
baby trees growing out of stumps.

What else have you come across?

Make a silly hat to wear to a party or at the dinner table.

Just make slits on each side of a paper plate in which to tie strings to keep the hat on.

Glue all kinds of things on the plate—feathers, flags, toy boats, flowers, streams of crepe paper, etc.

* If your friends make silly hats too, you could go for a parade around the block.

Imagine these sounds—
Can you imagine the sound of waves on huge rocks?
Can you imagine the quiet lapping of water against a rowboat?
What about how an old house creaking on a stormy night?
Isn't it scary?

Play Toss-and-Catch with anyone in the family who isn't doing anything special.
A ping-pong ball is good to use
or
what about using an inflated balloon?

Visit a conservation project, one where they protect:
water
soil
or
a forest and wildlife.
Wouldn't it be great if they let you go with them when they take bird or animal counts?

Go to the water fountain at the shopping plaza
and
watch the water fall into the pool.
Does the water fountain have any other visitors besides you?
Are there any birds?
any insects?
dogs?
Look at the mother holding her child so that its little toes are cooled in the water.

Everybody go to the city-wide inter-denominational music festival.
What a treat it would be to see and hear people singing songs from all over the world.
You could hear wonderful African songs

Arabic songs
Mexican songs
Irish songs
many other kinds of songs.

Doesn't it make you feel that all of us—wherever we live—are sisters and brothers?

Eat some strawberries you picked all by yourself.

In the early summer, when it's strawberry season, go to a farmer who grows strawberries
and
(for just a little bit of money)
pick all the strawberries you want—
RIGHT FROM THE VINE!

There is one serious problem about all this though—once you start eating strawberries—IT'S HARD TO STOP!

Walk down and around your block
and
pick up all the litter you can find
put the litter in a bag
and
drop it in the trash can.

Doesn't this make you feel good inside?

Listen to the swallows chirping and twittering
and

See how they dart around and glide. (Wouldn't you love to have the swallow take a message to your friend who moved down south?)

If you have nothing special to do—
Play a recorded story.
Did you ever hear:
"Train to the Zoo"?
"Winnie the Pooh"?
"Let's Be Firemen"?
"Muffin in the City"?
or "Muffin in the Country"?

Pretend you are a mountain climber
and
climb up a great big, tall heaping mountain of snow
and then
slide all the way down.

Listen to your sister practice her flute.
Isn't the flute a nice instrument to play?
Would you like to play a flute someday?
or
Would you like to play a different instrument such as a piano or a saxophone?
How would you like to play a TROMBONE?

At night—when it's pitch black outside—
Go into your backyard and chase fireflies.
Isn't it fun to see how they dart about and
how their lamps glow so bright?
BUT—
WHEN THOSE LAMPS GO OUT—you can't tell where they are
UNTIL
they decide to play a joke and wink at you!

Make some dried apples.
Ask a grown-up to help you:

Take the core and seeds out of the apples. Slice the apples about 1/2-inch thick.
Can you string the rings several inches apart on string or on a stick (such as a broomstick?)
Can you hang the string outdoors to dry in the sun by yourself?
In about one week you'll have your home-made dried apples!

Help your dad make a shelf for your books, toys, and collection of stones.
Doesn't it make you feel grown up to help
measure the wood,
saw the wood,
nail the pieces of wood together,
and
paint the wood just the color you want?

If you had a grown-up friend who had a raft
and
made everything nice and safe for you
Don't you think it would be even more fun than floating on a canoe?
an ocean liner?
or
some fancy yacht?

Get out that old, old gadget that was once used to wash dishes, a kind of "dish mop."
Dip it in paint.
Swirl and wiggle it around on paper.
And you'll have a pretty "dish mop" masterpiece that you and others can enjoy.

Think about how nice it would be to:
sleep in an apple tree or on a ship at sea
play on a pile of hay with your cats
or
with woolly lambs on a cloud in the sky.
Would you like to have golden wings strong enough to carry you over snow-capped mountains far away, higher than the tallest trees?

Make a pile of:
those old games you played a million times which are too babyish for you now

the books you know by heart already and no longer want
your jeans that you can hardly squeeze into
your shoes that pinch you
and
why not recycle them with a friend or the neighbors
or
give them to Goodwill, the Salvation Army, the Night People, or the homeless
or
(if you need the money) use them in a garage sale or the nearby flea market?

Watch the bricks being laid for a walkway or a new building.
Come back day after day to see how much work has been done since you were last there.

Help your sister make candy apples even if it isn't Halloween.
Be sure to make enough for the whole family.

Help pull out weeds from the garden; but be sure to pull them out by their roots.
Do you know why?

Keep your eyes wide open for that little bird that knocks on wood. Yes!—It's the woodpecker.
Do you know why this bird was named the woodpecker? It's because it pecks on wood. Do you know why it pecks on wood? It pecks the bark of the tree looking for insects' babies to eat. The woodpecker is really a bird carpenter!
If you walk up to the tree where it's pecking, it probably won't fly away. It'll just hurry around to the other side of the tree and play peekaboo with you! See for yourself!

Look out your window
and
watch cars going by

red cars
blue cars
green cars
white ones.
Do you wonder where they're all going?

Play "I'm thinking of a word that sounds like________."

For example:

I'm thinking of a word that sounds like "feet."
When suppertime comes, it's time to________.

I'm thinking of a word that sounds like "hat."
I say "meow," so I'm a_________.

I'm thinking of a word that sounds like "red."
When I'm sleepy, I go to_________.

Now you make up some.

Go with an adult to an outdoor movie house to see *Pinocchio* (or some other good children's movie).
Wouldn't it be super if you could buy some buttered popcorn too?

Have a "treasure hunt" in your house.
Hunt for things colored blue, yellow, etc.
Hunt for things that are straight, curved, square, etc.
Hunt for things that are dark or light
things that are high or low
sharp things or dull things
Did you ever think that your house had so many different kinds of things in it?
Someday have a treasure hunt outdoors and hide things for your friends to find.
Did you ever have a treasure hunt hiding things that are hard to find—but not impossible—things like:
a fallen feather

an acorn
a key that isn't used any more?
Do you have a toy ring you can hide?

Have a tasting party.
What can you taste that is sour—oh, so sour?
a lemon
or
lime?
Now find something that is bitter, like a radish.
Can you eat one without making a face?
What about a sweet taste? That's easy—isn't it?

Draw pictures of things that go FAST.
Draw pictures of things that go SLOW.
Can you draw some things that go FAST and SLOW?

Take a "Mile" walk by
placing the heel of one shoe so that it touches the toe of the other at every step.
It's not easy—is it?

Play "Blind Man's Bluff."
You've really never ever played "Blind Man's Bluff"?
Well—it's lots of fun and you don't need anything but a big hanky or a scarf to tie around someone's eyes.
Then the "blind man" uses his or her ten fingers to touch a
person
and
tries to guess who is touched.
If someone has braids, it's a little easy.
If someone is very tall, it's easy—or
if someone is very short.
If someone is fat or skinny, it's easy.
(When the "blind" person guesses the right name of the person, it's that person's turn to be the "blind man.")

Try to visit:
a Christmas Eve service
a baptism
an Easter service
a Jewish synagogue
a Catholic mass
a rural church
a city mission
a Muslim mosque
a Mormon temple
a convent
a storefront church
Look at their different buildings, the murals and paintings on their walls.
Do they all have stained-glass windows? statues?
Do some of the people wear different kinds of clothing?

Cut heavy wool scraps or old nylon stockings into long, skinny pieces.
Attach them to a doorknob and get a grown-up to teach you how to braid.
Just think how nice it is to know how to braid your hair or your sister's hair.
Also, someday you may want to make a braided rug for your room—wouldn't that be something!

*It's good to keep the braid on a doorknob so that it's always there (and out of the way) until you feel like braiding again.

Tell the family about how you got caught
in the rain
about your stomachache
the movie you saw
your trip to the zoo
what you did at your friend's house.
Anything else?

If you have a camera, take pictures of:
your favorite flower
the squirrel on your front lawn
your cat sleeping
your favorite animal at the zoo
the tree in your backyard in summer, fall, winter, and spring

* Be sure you put the dates on the back of your pictures and put them in your photograph album as soon as you can.

If someone big is watching you—
learn to use a cross-cut saw.
You might need help to make the first few strokes, but once you get started—you can keep going yourself.
How about sawing the wood into different sizes for a collection of building blocks?
Learn how to use sandpaper
and
if you want to paint your blocks—learn how to use paint the right way.
All this can make you feel really BIG!

For a friend who has a birthday and has just about every toy in the world—
why not buy a jar of honey?

If you want to be "big," be sure to learn your right hand from your left hand.
You can learn it fast if you say or sing "Looby Lou."
It goes like this:

I put my right hand in.
(Have someone tell you which is your right hand.)

I put my right hand out.
I give my right hand a
shake, shake, shake
and turn myself around.

Then, do the same thing using your left hand. Then, your right and left feet.

Another way to learn your right from your left is to put a decal, a ribbon, or pipe cleaner rings on your right hand—and then on your left hand later.

Go to the piano and play
one note
and
the next note
and
the next note.
Can you get someone to walk or dance to your music while you play?
Now try this:
Can you make the sound of a soft, steady rain? thunder?
Do you think you could make up a little ditty on the piano?

Look around at the houses near you.
Isn't it strange that the houses near you look bigger than the houses that are farther away?

If you ever come across a dead butterfly or other bugs already dead,
save them and start a prize BUG COLLECTION.

If you cut a banana in half
and
If you spread peanut butter over the banana half
and
if you set raisins into the peanut butter
You will have "Ants on a Log" to devour!

There are lots of things to listen to in your house, but did you ever hear:

Your furnace going on and off?
The rumble of the water pipes?
The humming of the refrigerator?
Did you ever hear your floor boards squeak?

In the summer, when the sun is strong and it's so hot—beat the heat with your garden hose.

Can you make it rain with your hose?
Can you gently squirt yourself and your friends with your hose?
Look at your little sister's bare toes. They need sprinkling like a thirsty rose—don't they?
What about your thirsty dog, can you give her some water?

* While you're at it—would you like to make a rainbow from the fine spray of your hose?

You can, if you make sure the sun shines behind you while you spray a fine mist.
Aren't the rainbow colors pretty?

Make a potato person by poking toothpicks into a potato for legs and arms.

If there are any smaller potatoes, why not make a whole potato family?
Don't waste the potatoes when you're done. They're great for boiling and mashing and eating!

Get together all your friends and go galloping like ponies down the block.

Make a pretty print on cloth or paper.
All you need to do is take the ends of sticks, bolts, nuts, screws, or just nails
press them onto a pad made of lots of paper towels soaked in watercolor paint
and then press the coated end on a piece of paper or cloth.
You can also use different shapes cut from carrots, potatoes, and corks.
(You may not be very good at first, but you'll get better as you go along.)

Visit the fire station with a grown-up. (It's a good idea to make an appointment for this first because firefighters are very busy people.)
They would be glad to let you try on a firefighter's hat.
Maybe you will be able to see a firefighter slide down the firepole.
Wouldn't it be a real treat if they let you go on a fire truck and stand where they stand?
If they're not too busy, they'll be so glad to tell you about the dangerous work they do.
Would you like to be a firefighter someday?

* Someday your parents may be able to take you to visit a fire tower in a forest and talk to a fire ranger too!

Be a color magician.
Get out three crayons from your coloring box—red, yellow, and blue.

When you mix red and yellow, what color do you get?
  (orange)
When you mix yellow and blue, what color do you get?
  (green)
Now mix red and blue, and you get purple.
  See—now you have six colors from three colors!

Go to bed where it's safe and warm
and
listen to thunder crashing and rain.
Is lightning flashing too?
  Isn't it scary?

Think about what you'd like to be when you "grow up."
Would you like to be:
  a construction worker?
  a bus driver?
  a train conductor?
  a cook?
  a baseball star?
  a firefighter?
  a window washer?
  a hairdresser?
  an astronaut?
  a teacher?
  a doctor?
  a lawyer?
  a sanitation worker?
  a candy-store owner?
Pretend you are the one you'd like to be.

If you can get permission from the workers,
look down the great big hole in the street.
See all the pipes that are under the city:
  pipes to bring in water for the laundry, the beauty parlor, all the faucets in the city.
  pipes to get rid of the dirty water from the sewers, the gutters, and toilets.

pipes to bring in gas for the hot water heaters and refrigerators, the furnaces and stoves to bake cookies and cake.

And—

See all the electricity wires for traffic lights and the rooms for all the houses in the city.

Did you ever think that so much goes on below the street?

Look at that poor weeping willow on the lawn next door.

Why does it seem so sad?

Could it be that the bluejay decided to choose a different tree for its nest this year?

Help with your baby sister's bath.

Can you help wash her down with soap and water?

Can you oil and powder her?

Can you help dress her for the night?

Will Mother or Dad let you pull her by the arms and raise her up a little from her mat—just before she's tucked in—with a kiss for the night?

Go to the biggest mirror you have in your house.

Can you make yourself:

proud?
sad?
happy?
silly?
angry?
scary?

Can you dance in front of your mirror?

Can you draw a picture of you?

If you had a rearview mirror, could you look at something that was behind you?

Could you walk backward using the mirror to see where you're going?

IF you don't have a mirror—try to look at yourself on some ice.

OR

Look at yourself in a puddle of water.

Look carefully. Do you see more wonders in the puddle than in the mirror?

If you have a fireplace—
Sit in front of it (but not too close).
Don't do anything at all
and
just toast yourself like a marshmallow.

Go see the free programs sponsored by the city parks department.
You might see a puppet show
a dance program
a storyteller
What a treat!

Check out the sidewalks around town.
If you get down very close—you may find shells or colorful pebbles right there in the concrete.
Did you ever see shimmering mica in the sidewalk?

See if you can be an "adventurer" in everything you see and do. How much there is to explore. For example:
If you find a pile of leaves, look under it to see what's going on.
If you hear a bee buzzing, what flower is it on?
If you have a pretty flower, take it apart to see what's in it.
If Mother is making soup for dinner, would you like to see what goes into it?
Even if you are putting on your shoes, what are they made of?

Climb the backyard rope ladder. (Even if it's not a very high one, grown-ups may shudder to watch you. But you're pretty surefooted, aren't you?)

Watch a bird fly down and eat a big fat worm.

Do you think birds like worms as much as you like a glass of milk and strawberry pie?

Eat your breakfast really early.
Go outside
and
watch the dew sparkle on the grass.

See how many cartwheels you can do at one time without falling down and hurting yourself.

Go through old books,
old newspapers
and
old magazines
and
cut out pictures of things that begin with an "a" sound.
Then cut out pictures of things that begin with a "b" sound.
Keep going like this through the whole alphabet.
Then,
paste the pictures in the alphabet book where they belong.

Act out heavy, heavier, and heaviest with a pile of books.
Act out small, smaller, and smallest by sharpening a pencil.
Act out tall, taller, and tallest with blocks.
Can you act out loud, louder, and loudest with your voice, saying "I love you"?

Invent a new shuffleboard game by drawing lines with chalk on the basement floor
or
in the driveway
and
use a broom and a pie tin or pot lid to play the game.

If you pound some nails into a board and wind string or colored yarn in and around the nails, you can make some really pretty designs. An artist doesn't always need paint to make a pretty picture!

Hide behind the curtains till someone finds you.
Shhh Shhhh

Have a "yogurt party" for just you or with your friends.
Do you know that millions of people all over the world eat yogurt?
And there are so many different kinds too!
Like:
vanilla yogurt
honey yogurt
strawberry yogurt
pineapple yogurt
And
Do you know that yogurt can be used for:
"dips"
salad dressing
to top potatoes
Really though—the very best yogurt is FROZEN YOGURT "ICE CREAM"!

Go with your mother and little brother to the barber shop when he gets his first haircut.

Take the old oatmeal or grits box and some spoons or sticks
and
drum away.
BOOM
BOOM
BOOM!

Get out your apron—
tie up your sleeves
and
try this recipe for Maple Delight:

Needed: 1 glass milk
1 tablespoon maple syrup
1 jar with lid

What to do: Put milk and maple syrup in jar.
Put lid on jar tight.
Shake well.
Serve.

* Make a chocolate milkshake the same way, using one tablespoon of chocolate syrup instead of maple.

Get out your ball and jacks
and play a couple of games with your friends.

If you live in the city, make a map of the block where you live.
Can you show where you live?
your neighbors to the right and left of you?
the houses across the street?
the corner store?
the mailbox?
What else?

If you live in the country—
Can you show:
your house?
your nearest neighbors' farm?
where you go shopping?
Are there any valleys?
streams?
fields?
wood lots?

Is there a library where you can go for books and weekly story hours?

Does one of your friends have a bulldog?
And another friend, a collie?
Does their fur feel the same?
Does a pony feel like a horse?
Do the feathers of a chicken feel like those of a pigeon?
Does walnut wood feel like pine wood?
Do oats feel like wheat?
How much our fingers can tell us—can't they?

Get hold of clothes that no one needs or wants any more and
play "grown-up."
Try to collect:
old hats, scarves, and gloves
pocketbooks, filled with odds
and ends, ties, belts, and vests
high-heeled shoes and boots
long skirts, half-slips, shawls, and veils
sparkly jewelry, dangling earrings,
bracelets, compacts and empty lipsticks
eyeglass frames
and
broken watches
etc.

Close your eyes and think of what it would be like if:
you could never hear anything—nobody talking
no birds singing
you couldn't see anyone
trees
books
you had one arm or one foot instead of two
you lived in a house where there was no love and nobody to help you with anything.
It would be pretty rough—wouldn't it?
Do you think it would be a wonderful thing if you could help others?

Look around and see if you can find a dead tree in your neighborhood.

Then stop a couple of minutes to look at it and think about all the good things it did when it was alive.

Did birds build their nests in it?

If you look at its highest branches, is there a clump of tangled leaves and twigs?

(It may have been a squirrel's home.)

Were its flowers pretty in the spring?

When it was so hot outside, did its shade make people feel better?

If it was an apple tree, a pear tree, or a peach tree—did people enjoy the fruits?

Now take a very close look at the tree.

Do you see centipedes, beetles, and bugs living there?

Look! There's a seedling nearby for a new baby tree!

Draw pictures of places you've never been, like:

a treetop
the moon
a rain forest
deep under the ocean

What other places can you think of?

Think of the wonderful things we have, wonderful things that you can't buy in a store.

We have eyes to see the beautiful shapes and colors of things.

We have ears to hear the soft, secret sounds of nature.

We have a nose to sniff the good smells of the seasons.

Our tongues enjoy the taste of food.

We have hands to feel the bark of a tree and the cool roundness of pebbles.

And

We have curiosity to make us wonder and find out about things.

Best of all: WE HAVE HEARTS TO BE KIND TO ALL LIVING THINGS.

Just look about at your father, your mother, your sisters and brothers, and the new little baby.
Do you see a lot of love there?
Doesn't it seem like love and family go together?
Other things seem to go together too, like:
gardens with flowers
zoos with elephants
a knife with a fork
How about ball and bat? That's a good one—isn't it?
What other things seem to go together?

Do you live near a river or can you get to see one?
Look at the quiet and peaceful river.
See how it sparkles so brightly in the sun.
Doesn't it look as if someone has thrown diamonds on the water as it flows along?

Enjoy the feel of:
your pillow and how fluffy it is
cold snow on your hands
your kitten's fur
squeezing a marshmallow
a bedtime kiss

Scoop up some worms and put them in a jar.
Punch a couple of holes in the lid.
Add a handful of earth
some grass
or
leaves.
Then watch the worms make tunnels and leave their round castings behind.

* After a day or so, empty out the jar so every worm can go back home where it belongs.

Just think what life would be like if:
we didn't have electric lights
we didn't have cars or trucks
no one ran the farms and we didn't have people to milk the cows
or feed the chickens
we didn't have running water—just like in the old, old days!
Hmmmm!

Get out the family's tent
help set it up
and
let it be a lions' den.

Call your best friend on the telephone and talk about anything.

Plan a visit to your grandmother, the one who knows so many great stories about plants and animals. Here's one you can listen to over and over again—

"I dropped a seed into the earth. It grew, and the plant was mine. It was a wonderful thing, this plant of mine. I did not know its name, and the plant did not bloom. All I know is that I planted something apparently as lifeless as a grain of sand and there came forth a green and living thing unlike the seed, unlike the soil in which it stood, unlike the air into which it grew. No one could tell me why it grew, nor how. It had secrets all its own, secrets that baffle the wisest men; yet this plant was my friend. It faded when I withheld the light, it wilted when I neglected to give it water, it flourished when I supplied its simple needs. One week I went away on a vacation, and when I returned the plant was dead; and I missed it. Although my little plant had died so soon, it had taught me a lesson; and the lesson is that it is worthwhile to have a plant."

(*The Nature Study Idea*, L. H. Bailey)

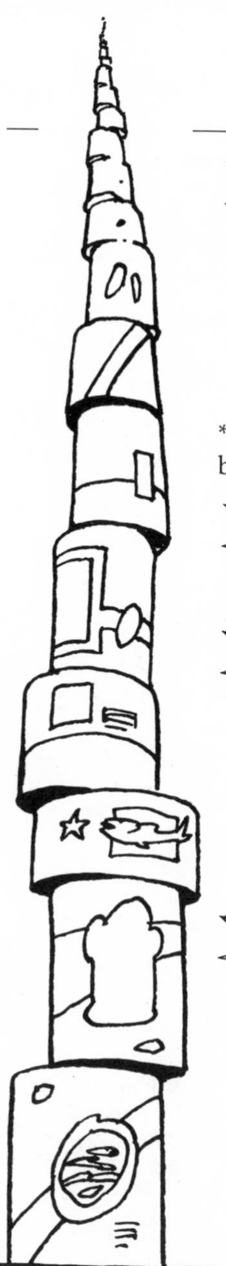

Hear what sounds paper can make.
Listen:
How does it sound when you tear it?
when you cut it with scissors?
when you crumble it?
Can you hear it when it drops?

* If your eyes were closed, could you tell what was being done with the paper?

Practice soccer with a friend. Maybe you'll be able to make the team someday!

Get permission to take out a bunch of cans from the pantry
and
make a huge tower with them.
(You'll find that cans can make towers just as tall and as good as store-bought blocks can. Yes!)

Hunt all over for any of these old unused, unwanted papers.
Use that wonderful brain you have and think about one or two ways each can be recycled.
THEN—undertake some of them.

crepe paper
tissue paper
advertising pamphlets
wax paper
mail order catalogs
newspapers
gift-wrapping paper
shelf paper
corrugated paper
cardboard filler from packaged shirts
magazines

Did you think of cutting out pictures from old magazines?
You can make a collage out of them.

OR

How about cutting out the white parts of the shelf paper and using them to write little notes on?

(If you think hard enough—and if you ask your friends to help you—you can get a list of things a mile long!)

Take a ferryboat ride across the river
back and forth
back and forth
back and forth
from one shore to the other.
See the freighters
the barges
the cruise boats.
Are there any fishing boats out?
See the tugboats
chugging
puffing
chugging and
puffing.
Do you see seagulls?
Do you feel the water spray on you?
IS THAT A DUCK PASSING BY?

Go outdoors just to look for any flower or any leaf that has a fresh, wonderful smell and bring it inside for everyone else to enjoy.

Put a can outdoors to collect rainwater.
Be a meteorologist and measure (or ask someone to help you measure) how much it rained.
Do you know that this rainwater is just perfect for watering your indoor plants?

Look about at all the great things there are that are free to enjoy—

the golden sun
blooming cherry trees
the song of birds
a small violet
Did you ever see corn growing?
rain
butterflies
freshly cut grass
the hum of a bee
a blue stream and the blue sky
bees in purple clover
little breezes
the baby's tiny feet
ANYTHING ELSE?

Find out what your "state tree" is.
Here are a few state trees to start you off:
sugar maple—Vermont
pecan—Texas
magnolia—Mississippi

* Ask an adult if he or she can add to these. (You will probably have to get a book of state trees from the library.)

If there are tours to:
a Mormon temple or tabernacle
or
a Buddhist monastery
or
a little New England church—
wouldn't you love to see them?
See how the buildings are so different outside.
Are the paintings on the walls and the statues different?
Are the gardens around the buildings different too?
Do some of the people wear different kinds of clothing?

Try some of these silly questions on your friends and see if you can get some very silly answers.

If an elephant were to sit on a fence, what time would it be? (Time to get a new fence)

Three big women went walking under one umbrella, but none of them got wet. Why? (Because it wasn't raining)

What is the best thing you can put on pumpkin pie? (Your teeth)

Why did the rooster cross the road? (To get to the other side)

Why do birds like to fly south for the winter? (Because it's too far to walk)

What is a bird after he is four days old? (Five days old)

What makes more noise than a pig does? (Two pigs)

How do you greet a three-headed monster? (Hello. Hello. Hello. How are you? How are you? How are you?)

What do your shoes become when you step into a puddle? (Wet)

What is the hardest thing about learning to skate? (The ice)

What falls down but never gets hurt? (Snow)

What do you lose every time you get up? (Your lap)

What animal can jump higher than a house? (Any animal. A house can't jump.)

What weighs more? A pound of cookies or a pound of butter? (They both weigh the same.)

What gets bigger the more you take away? (A hole)

Dawdle.

Sometimes don't you get sick and tired of hearing:

"Hurry up!"

"Hurry up!"

"Don't be so slow!"

or

"Come in right now, this very minute!"

Wouldn't it be great if sometimes you could just dawdle?

If you're getting dressed, why can't you dawdle?

What's wrong with dawdling as you brush your teeth?

When you're outside plopping pebbles in puddles, why can't you dawdle and come in any old time?

Do you always have to eat up your lunch one, two, three?

Why can't you dawdle especially when you're eating your crackers and jelly?

When you're sitting in your secret hiding place and dreaming of riding kangaroos
climbing to the top of a giraffe's neck
or
dancing with a bear
why should that be called dawdling?
Do you think that sometimes "big" people don't understand children?

When it's windy out, go fly your kite.
(If your backyard has trees or wires about—then try to get to an open meadow or a parking lot that may be closed for the weekend.)
How would you like to be a kite and look out at everything—
roofs
and
trees
and
telephone poles?

But—then again—IF you were a kite, you'd never be able to see
an ant dragging a leaf
and
dandelions
and
caterpillars.

Get out your paint set and paint a picture of
your puppy
a zebra
marshmallows
dandelions, daffodils, or daisies
a big snowfall
a cowboy hat
a mouse
an ice cream cone
Can you draw an old woman living in a shoe?
Can you draw it "raining cats and dogs"?

* One of the best parts to painting is that nobody cares what you paint but YOU! So that makes it easy!

Walk to the corner of the street where you live
and
just listen to the sounds the cars make.
When they start—do you hear sounds like
jerks?
chunk, chunk?
or
coughing, like they
sort of had a cold?
And
When they go off—do you hear sounds like
rattling?
banging?
knock-knockings?
or
purring like a cat?

Pretend you are a flower.
How would it feel to be warmed by the sun?
if someone put his or her nose up to you and smelled you?
if a bee took nectar from you?
How would you feel if bugs crawled all over you?

See if you or you and your friends can think of things that begin with letters of the alphabet.
For example:
A (ant)
B (book)
C (cat)
etc.
Now, see how many foods you can think of that begin with the letters of the alphabet. It may be hard for you to think of foods for all the letters. And—you may not be able to think of one for "X." You may have to skip that letter because there are few foods in the whole wide world that begin with an X.
Here are some to try:
A (apple)
B (bread)
C (cake)
Now you do the rest . . .

Help your little sister or brother play happily alone for a while.
Just tie a lot of things to where he or she is (whether in the stroller or in a bassinet) with a string short enough not to pose a hazard to the child.
Things like:
wooden spoons (very good for banging)
a doll
an empty oatmeal box, etc.
The baby can then drop and get them back again easily.
Tying the things up is especially good because you don't have to stoop and bend to pick them up! Isn't that nice?

Make a FAMILY NEWSPAPER.
You can be the editor-in-chief collecting
things to "write" about or draw, things like:
the baby's new tooth
Aunt Sally's wedding
the new kitten
Mom's new job, etc.
Do you think Grandpa—who lives
so far away from you—would
enjoy getting a copy of the
FAMILY NEWSPAPER?

Do you know you can play
with a snowman in the
hot heat of the summer?
You really can!
All you need to do is to get hold of a pillow.
Then, slip a pillowcase over it.
Tie some cord across the top of it to make the snowman's head.
Attach bits of colored paper or cloth to the head to make eyes, nose, and a mouth.
Put on a hat.
And there you are!

Play "wedding" with your friends.
For a wedding you need a boy and a girl (If you don't have a boy, another girl can "be" the boy.)
You need someone to be a holy person—like a priest, a minister, or a rabbi.
You need some flowers. Dandelions are just fine.
You need a ring. A twister is good to use, or pretend you have a ring even if you don't.
And
Of course, you need lots of people for dancing around the newlyweds.

* If you have a wagon, someone can fly you off to Hawaii for a honeymoon.

Get out a fork and eat the cherry pie you got for being good all day.

If the light is good behind the living room couch, get out a supply of your favorite books and "read."
Isn't it fun to be by yourself sometimes?

Enjoy the rain.
Think of all the wonderful things you can do when it rains.
Get out your raincoat and rubbers and go for a walk in the rain. (Don't the raindrops look like jewels on the leaves?)
Can you catch a raindrop on your tongue?
Isn't it a wonderful feeling to have your face washed by the rain?
Watch a raindrop hit a puddle of water.
Do you see the little circle it makes?
then a bigger circle
then a bigger circle around that one?
Do you see rain gushing out of a neighbor's drainpipe?
Have a great adventure in a pool of rainwater where twigs and grass are boats
and
people are always brave and good.
Isn't it hard to understand why some people don't like the rain?

Look out at the window on a cold winter day.
Does the window have a pattern of frost that looks like lace?
Will you be allowed to draw pictures on the frost?

Shine everybody's shoes. (Do you know anyone who wouldn't really appreciate it?)

Build a bridge by putting a flat board across a mud hole and walk across it.
Careful!

Dance with the kitchen broomstick! It could be as much fun as dancing with a real person!

Go for a subway ride underneath the big city.
See all the people!
young
old
poor
rich
standing
sitting
of all different colors
some with smiles
some without smiles
some reading the paper
some just staring into space and thinking
BUT ONE THING IS THE SAME—THEY'RE ALL GOING SOMEWHERE!

See how many of these things you can do.
And then see if your friend can tell what you're doing.
stand
sit
slide
jump
skip
bend
squiggle
gallop
twist
touch
swing
kneel
flop

crawl
stretch
twirl
leap
and
soar like an eagle
twirl like a top
wave good-bye
rub your tummy
throw a kiss

Watch a slithery garden snail inching its way among the vegetables.
Isn't it really quite wonderful that it can do this with no feet, no arms, and no tail?

Get out a blanket and pillow and take a little nap under a tree.
(Maybe when you wake up, there'll be a pretty butterfly on your shoulder—
or
an ANT!)

Think about all the things you HAVE to do instead of all the things you'd LIKE to do, like:
Wouldn't you rather eat your supper outside sitting on a big stone instead of in the dining room chair?
or
sleep on a haystack with your kittens instead of in your bed?
Life is sometimes hard for children, isn't it?

Watch a praying mantis kneeling in the tall grass.
Do you think the praying mantis is religious—it seems to pray so much.
Don't let this mantis fool you!
It may LOOK as if it's praying, but it's pretty clever. This smart praying mantis is just

waiting
 and
watching
 TO POUNCE ON AN INSECT TO DEVOUR!

Did you ever play a game with some other children and it was hard to decide who should be "it"?

Well—here's a way lots of children many years ago and even now—decide. They recite a "counting out" rhyme. The person who is to start the game is chosen in this way.

As the rhyme is said, a different person is pointed to after each word. When you come to the last word "mo," that person is "it" or starts the game. Try it:

Eeny, meeny, miny, mo.
Catch a tiger by the toe.
If he hollers, let him go.
Eeny, meeny, miny, mo.

Here's another starter:
One, two, three.
Mother caught a flea.
Out in the middle
Of the dark blue sea.

And another:
Ickabocker, ickabocker, ickabocker, boo!
Ickabocker, soda cracker, out goes Y-O-U.

Try keeping your balance on stilts.
It isn't easy, is it?
But if you can and get good at it—
Isn't it a great feeling to be the tallest of all your friends?
(Also, isn't it a little easier to peek into your windows?)

See how many times you can tap a balloon in the air with one hand.
With the other hand.

Get out a pinwheel and whirl it around up and down the street.

Look at your brand new baby brother.
Do you think he would like you to read him a story?
Would he like you to tell him what you did today?
Would he like to see your doll?
(Strange! He doesn't seem to be interested in anything but eating and sleeping. Could he be too little?)

Wrestle with your best friend.
Poke each other (easy though!).
Punch each other (gently!).
Roll in the grass (carefully!).
Don't be rough or YOU'LL BE SORRY!

Roast chestnuts you bring home from the store.

Just know that any way you roast them is just great—
whether in the oven
the fireplace
or
over an outdoor fire.
(Lots of people think this way is the most fun. Do you?)

If there's a big parade downtown, go to watch it.
Wouldn't you love to see the President of the United States in a parade? WOW!

Join your neighbors in a sing-along in their backyard.
Did you ever take part in a banjo or guitar sing-along?

Learn to whistle.

Wouldn't it be fun to be able to whistle?

Try it!

You've set your mouth just right. But the whistle doesn't seem to want to come out.

Did it get stuck?

Do you think the whistle sound got swallowed?

IT MUST HAVE!

Test this out: The tips of our tongues are good for tasting sweet and salty foods.

The middle parts of our tongues are for sour and salty foods.

And for bitter foods, we have the back parts of our tongues.

Watch the paper carrier ride down the street on a bicycle

and

see how he or she throws the evening news toward someone's front door.

Would you like to be a news carrier someday too?

Ask someone to take you down to the basement to see the pipes that take the clean water from deep under the ground up to your kitchen

and

the pipes that take the dirty dish water far down into the sewer.

* If you check under your kitchen sink—guess what you'll find!

Go walking or jogging with your mother. Can you keep up with her?

Don't you feel good after you've walked (or jogged)?

Tie a long ribbon to the end of a stick—

and

Run with it down the block
or
Just stick it in the ground and watch the ribbon fly in the wind.

Have everyone around you think of "go-together" words, like:
bat and ball
soap and water
shoes and socks
What else?

If you're not too, too big—
Can you climb with your feet
up the front of your dad by holding his hands?
(It's not easy, but if you CAN do it—it's great fun!)

Enjoy the sweet scent of freshly baked biscuits drifting in from the kitchen.
Doesn't it smell so-o-o-o good?

Get out your wind-up cars or dragons to play with.

Turn over a little part of your garden and count all the worms you see.

See if you can blow up a balloon without getting red in the face.

Be a different kind of artist.
Make a picture by dribbling glue over colored paper or cardboard.
Sprinkle some sand over the glue.
When the paper or cardboard is tipped over, the extra sand will fall off
and
WHAT IS LEFT IS YOUR PICTURE!

Roll an orange or a lemon across the room using a pencil to push it along.
Do it just by yourself
or
Do it with a friend and see who can get it across the room faster.

Cut up colored paper into a zillion pieces
and a zillion different shapes.
Paste them onto a gigantic piece of cardboard.
Now don't you think this is a very good piece of art?

Ask a grown-up to collect things around the house that are the same in one way—
but different in another way.
For example, things like:
an apple and an orange
a coat and a sweater
pictures of a lion and a monkey
Do you know how these things are alike and how they are different?

Plant a dried bean in a small can full of earth.
Put it on the windowsill
and
watch it grow.
(But don't forget to water it!)

Watch the butterfly on the yellow flower.
Is it sleeping or feeding on the flower's sweetness?
Isn't it too bad that the butterfly will fly away and you won't be able to find out?

Pick up an acorn.
Did you know that an acorn has a little cap?

Acorns are great for counting
for making into dolls
or
for planting in the soil.

If the traveling bookmobile is in your neighborhood, get down there and pick out a book to take home to read.
(Doesn't it make you feel sort of "special" to have the books come to you instead of your going to the books?)

Draw things with a compass, like suns and moons,
hoops and wheels
and lots of money.

Think of things that have one wheel.
Can you think of what has two wheels?
three
or
four wheels?

Swat at some mosquitoes near the picnic table and tell them to go some other place!

What would you do if you had a million dollars?
Would you buy a castle?
What about getting a rocket to go to the moon?
How about buying a toy store?
What else would you do if you had a million dollars?

Think about this:
If you pick a lot of flowers, a lot of flowers will get lonesome for all those left behind.
But, if you pick only one flower, only one flower will get lonesome.
So—would you rather pick a lot of flowers
or
just one?

If you're in the country,
watch the farmer plow his
fields of wheat.
Would you like to be a farmer someday?

Race down the block as fast as you can.
Ask someone to count and see how long it takes.

Eat your lunch.
Can you eat your lunch with chopsticks?
or
what about a tongue depressor?

Look at your shoes.
Are there two of them? (Let's hope so! You'd look pretty funny if you walked around in just one shoe—
wouldn't you?)
Lots of other things come in two's, like:
two ears
two eyes
twins
What else?

Play this guessing game with your friend.
Say something special about an animal and see if your friend can guess what animal it is.
Try these out first:
What animal has a short, curly tail? (a pig)
What animal has a very long neck? (a giraffe)
What animal has a very bushy tail that's always such fun to watch? (a monkey)
Now, you make up some.

Play Tunnel Relay with your friend.
Get hold of four big boxes.
Fold in the tops and bottoms of each of the boxes.
Lay them on the ground end-to-end to form two tunnels—
NOW—see who can wiggle through the tunnels first!

If you want to be a knight in shining armor, get a big sheet of aluminum foil.
Put a hole in the middle of it so that the sheet can fit over your head (one side across your chest; the other side across your shoulders).
And you are now a knight in shining armor.

* If you need a shield to be a real knight, then just cut a circle out of a piece of cardboard and cover that with aluminum foil too.

Make a pull toy for your baby brother or sister from your big sister's hair rollers and a piece of string.
Or try
an empty spool of thread
a paper towel roll
or
a shoe.

Have a Dutch Shoe race with your friend.
You've never heard of a Dutch Shoe race?
Well—it's tons of fun and it's one where your dad might yell out, "Can't you have a quiet race of some other kind?"
Here's how it goes—
You and your friend put a shoe box on each foot.
With these on your feet, race by sliding the "shoes" along the ground from starting line to turning line and back.
The first one back wins!

Take a good look at that bird up there that seems to be flying like a helicopter.

Down
and
down it comes.
Oh, it's a maple tree seedpod!

Wiggle into your old snowsuit.
Hook up your boots.
Look for your missing mitten.
Tie your red scarf.
Get outside
and
Let the snowflakes dance around you.

Make a comb kazoo.
Just wrap a piece of tissue paper around a comb.
Hold the paper over the teeth of the comb while you place the comb against your lips.
Keep your lips open a bit, singing out nice and loud into the comb.
Doesn't it tickle your lips a little?

Take a look at all the beauty there is in nature.
Look at:
the vein of a leaf
the beauty of a melon that's split in half
seedpods
the lines in a seashell
the marvelous architecture of a bird's nest
an apple cut across the middle
See how the seeds of the apple rest—just like a star.

How would you like the birds to get you
and
gently carry you higher and higher into the sky
and crown you with stars?
Then you could be queen of the sky!

Watch workers dumping hot asphalt into holes in the street.
Is someone driving a gigantic roller to make the street nice and flat?

Make a super-smelling present from:
one orange, apple, lemon, or lime
whole cloves
ribbon or yarn
Here's what you do:
Push the little cloves into the unpeeled fruit and tie the fruit around with the ribbon or yarn.
Then, hang it wherever you wish.
Anyone in the world would enjoy such a sweet-smelling present.

Sit on your doorstep and look far out.
See how it's getting darker and darker every minute.
Do you see the moon now popping out right behind the big elm tree?
Look! The moon is smiling at you!

Hum a tune—any tune you like.
Hum it loud.
Hum it quietly.
Hum it low and deep.
Can anyone tell what you're humming?

Punch holes with a hole puncher in the old newspaper and make a snowstorm with the little circles.

Have a Discus Throw contest with your friend to see who can toss paper plates the farthest.
How good are you?

Think about how nature has given everyone a special kind of gift.

Do you know someone who sings well?
Isn't your friend good at modeling clay?
Some people are very quick with numbers.
What other gifts do you know of?
What about YOU? You have special gifts too.
What are they?

Look over the garden in the backyard.
See the potatoes growing.
Do you know how they grow? You don't, do you?
Isn't it quite wonderful that the potato knows something you don't know?

Go swinging on your fence railing.
Can you hang by your knees from your railing?
Can you look upside down, too?
How about turning in a circle on your railing?
What about just dangling your feet? That's easy, isn't it?

Have your friend tie his or her right leg to your left leg and
go for a "walk" together.
What fun you'll both have—as well as those who will be watching you!

Look at the videos of when you were a little baby.
(If you don't have videos, do you have pictures of yourself when you were a baby?)
What do you think of yourself?

Make a puzzle to give your friend as a birthday present.
To make a "house" puzzle (for example), find a big picture of a house in an old magazine and cut it out.
Glue the house onto cardboard. (Do you have a piece of cardboard from a new-shirt package?)
Then cut the house into two, three, four, or more pieces. Scatter

them about and put the house together again. Then give your friend this gift.

Practice playing basketball by putting up a hoop on the backyard tree. (An old milk crate will work well.)
Then you can pass the ball
dribble the ball
and
try to "make baskets" in the hoop.

Spin your top.
Let it whirl
twist
skip about
flip
and then
F L O P.

Take a ride on the seesaw with a friend.
(Be sure you sit in the right spot; otherwise it won't work right. And be sure to hold on tight!)

Eat a dill pickle. (If you don't have a dill pickle—do you have a green olive?)
Can you tell in words what it tastes like?

If you had a big pile of pennies, nickels, dimes, and quarters—could you sort them into piles?
If you had a great big pile of all the family's winter mittens, would you be able to sort them?
What about knives, forks, and spoons?
What about shoes? and socks?
If all the pots and pans were taken out of the cupboard, could you sort them too?

Get a few paper plates to draw on.
You can draw the face of everyone in the family
or
the face of each of your friends
a picture of your house
your pet or pets
anything in the whole world!

Pour water down a plastic tube and watch it go
down
down
down
until the water touches the ground.

On a hot summer night, go outdoors and listen to the sounds.
Can you make any of these sounds yourself?

Help tuck your sick grandfather in bed and sing a song for him.

See if you can tickle your mother's knee without her laughing or smiling.

Pull your friend in a wagon and then let your friend pull you.
* If you don't have a wagon, you can still have rides.
Just get a large box
tie a rope to it
and
PULL!
PULL!
PULL!

Build the tallest tower in the world with your blocks.
UPPS! The tower fell down!
Don't feel bad though. Lots of good things fall down, like:
Leaves—don't they fall down in the fall?
Apples fall down from trees, don't they?
What about petals from a flower?
What about rain?

Take your doll for a train ride.
First, find a shoe box.
Attach a string to it.
And
Pull away!
Do you think your doll would like a train ride around the whole world?

Water the garden if the soil is dry.
If you use a hose, use a gentle spray so that the water will soak in deep. (The roots of the plants need this water down deep to grow properly.)

Go for a swim.
If you can't swim yet, go wading in shallow water
or
just push water apart and move through it.

Play with an old sheet—
A big old sheet can make you a ghost.
Be a cloud.
If you put it over the back of a chair, it can be a cave.
Or
If you put it over the dining room table, it makes a wonderful tent for going camping.
What else can you do with a big old sheet?

Try to get permission to empty a box of salt into a box.
Draw pictures in the salt.
Practice "numbers" on it.
Can you write your name in salt?
Can you practice measuring salt with spoons and cups?

Spin around
and
around
and
around
without a stop.
Are you getting a little dizzy?
Is it hard to keep your balance?
Do you feel like a top that's just about to tumble over?

Spend the evening planning a hiking trip with the family.
(Of course, if you plan an overnight hiking-camping trip—that would be the best of all—wouldn't it?)

Choose a favorite story
or
a favorite poem.
Have someone read it or just tell it.
Then pretend to do whatever is done in the story.
Your rug can be a forest and your chair can be a castle.
You can do everything you want to do and be anyone you want to be.

Play football.
No, not real football yet.
But you can practice kicking a football
catching a football
and
passing it between legs—
can't you?

Go to the parade and listen to the band.
Listen especially to the deep, low tuba as it goes—
OOMPAH!
OOMPAH!
OOMPAH!

Listen. Is there a fly in the house?

Go skipping
hopping
and
jumping down the street.

Watch the birds eating.
How they love to eat their bugs, caterpillars, worms, and all kinds of berries and breadcrumbs.
Of course, birds do a lot of things all day, but sometimes doesn't it seem that all they do is eat?

Take a couple of minutes to make a rolling rattle.
Just get hold of an empty oatmeal box—
Put some beans
buttons
or
peach pits in it.
Seal the cover with tape.
And—that's it!
Now you can roll it along the floor
kick it like a football
or
beat it like a drum.

Get the family to help make lists of things that "go."
For example:
What "goes" on roads? cars, tow trucks, motorcycles, etc.
What "goes" in the sky? airplanes, helicopters, kites, etc.
What "goes" on water? rowboats, sailboats, canoes.
What "goes" on snow?
What "goes" on the farm?

Take a good, hard look at your fingers and think of all the wonderful things they can do for you.
They can hold crayons to help you draw.
They can hold a spoon to help you eat your soup.
They can help you enjoy the bark of a tree.
They can help you say "sh sh sh" when one of them is brought to your lips.
And, of course, fingers can give someone a good tickle!

Collect pictures of working people, like plumbers, doctors, teachers, construction workers, and others.
Cut them out of newspapers and magazines.
Can you also collect pictures of tools used by these workers and then match the tool with the worker?

If you can—
Get very close to a beetle.
It's so-o-o-o small—
But talk to the beetle and see if it will talk to you too.
Can the beetle smile, if you smile at it?
Can a beetle giggle too?
Look very, very close—Can a beetle wiggle its tongue?

Look down at your feet.
How many do you have?
How many do birds have?
What about the poor snail that has only one!

How many does your cat have? your dog? or a cow?
And ants—SIX feet!
And spiders—EIGHT!
What about the centipede—THIRTY FEET!
Aren't they lucky that they don't have to wear shoes!

Did you ever wonder what it would be like to be a ladybug?
You could climb up a blade of grass
and
if it's windy outside—
GET A FREE RIDE.

Go to the neighborhood park to watch
the softball game
the soccer game
or
a tennis match.

Watch the giant wrecking crane
swing its great big ball
and
knock down the walls of the warehouses
for the senior citizens' housing project that will be built soon.
C R A S H ! C R A S H !

Blindfold your dad and tell him to draw a house.
Then tell him to draw a garage for the house.
Then a car beside the garage.
When your dad is done, ask him to sign his name.
And then let him see what a great artist he is!

Watch the fresh fall of snow.
Now you can follow the footprints of some animals in the snow
and find out where they go!

Make a headdress from the garden flowers
and
be a queen for a day.

Think how lucky we are to have
bicycles to go on little trips
cars to go on bigger trips
trains to go on lots bigger trips
airplanes to go to faraway places—even around the world
and
ROCKETS THAT GO TO THE MOON.
(Wouldn't you love to ride on a rocket someday bound for the moon? or would you rather go to MARS?)

When you take a walk at night and you see warm, bright lights in peoples' houses
do you ever wonder what might be going on inside?
is someone reading the newspaper?
is someone writing a letter to a friend?
are children listening to someone telling them a story?
is a mother knitting a sweater for the baby?
do you think everyone feels safe and snug inside?

Help hang the wash outdoors.
Don't the dresses
the pants
and
pajamas
look so fresh and clean?
And the stockings—don't they look as if they're dancing in the wind?

Bounce a ball.
How many times can you bounce it before you miss?

Help your little baby sister walk when she takes her first steps. But you'll stay very close to her so that she doesn't fall down—won't you?

Blow bubbles.
Fill a small baby-food jar with a bit of liquid detergent and water and
blow bubbles with your old bubble wand.
(If you make the letter O with your thumb and finger, you will have a finger wand.)

* If you play with a friend, see how many bubbles you can each catch.

Throw newspaper balls and see how many times you can hit a circle on the wall. This is fun to do by yourself or with someone else.
* It's good to play in the house with paper balls because they can't hurt anybody—and, besides—when you're done playing with them, they can be popped right in your newspaper recycling bin!

Pretend you are a plane—
able to fly on a breeze
to fly over oceans
cities
mountains
trees
and then back to your house.

Be in a circus and do just what the ringmaster wants you to do "at the crack of the whip"!
Can you be a lion and roar and prance?
Can you be a donkey and refuse to budge?
What about flying like an eagle? Can you?
Can you gallop like a horse
and
dance awkwardly like an elephant?

Look up at the blue sky.
See the geese flying back from their long trip south.
See the little flowers coming up.
IT'S SPRING!
Doesn't it make you feel like singing and dancing?

See what happens when you put a thermometer:
in the sun
under a shady tree
on a radiator
in the basement
What happens when you put it in the refrigerator? in the freezer?

Enjoy the new, colorful mural at the entrance of the new school around the corner.
See, the mural shows children playing together—children who come from different countries and have different clothing and different skin colors.
Aren't they beautiful to look at? Wouldn't you like to have one for a friend?

Go out in the evening.
When you see the first star, say:
Star light, star bright,
The first star I see tonight,
I wish I may, I wish I might
Have the wish I wish tonight.

Then make a wish.

When you see the moon, say this little moon poem:
I see the moon
And the moon sees me.
And the moon sees somebody
I want to see.

Then make a wish.

Browse through the books in your room and pick out one special book.

Then snuggle up with a grown-up.

You get three wonderful things from this:

1) You get a good story.
2) You get a chance to talk about the story.
3) You'll be warm and close to each other. Isn't this worth about ten billion dollars?

Check outside your window. Do you see a bird's nest?

What a treat to watch the eggs hatch and the babies—little by little—learn to fly.

And then flutter away!

In the spring
get your breakfast
get dressed
and
go outdoors to hear the birds.
(Isn't it great to have a free serenade?)

Think of all the wonderful, wonderful things we get from cow's milk besides milk.

We get:

cream
yogurt
cheese
cottage cheese
cream cheese
butter
buttermilk
and (best of all) ice cream and whipped cream!

When you're out eating at a restaurant, don't mind asking for a "doggie bag" for the left-over food.

You can make another meal of it.
You can feed the birds or a dog with it.
Or why not feed it to the worms in your compost pile?

Look at the flowers in your garden.
Don't they look like a rainbow?

If you have a wood-burning stove in your living room or a fireplace that burns real wood
listen to the wood crackle when it burns.

Next time you see a dragonfly,
try to get close to it and look at its face.
(Doesn't the dragonfly look as if it's all eyes?)

See if you can
wiggle your eyebrows
or
wiggle your nose.
Now try to wiggle your eyebrows *and* wiggle your nose at the same time!

Rock back and forth in your rocking chair as though you were on a ship at sea.
Oh, what a storm!
Now the wind is calming down—at last!

Toss and roll a soft rubber ball that's attached to a string, which is tied to your hand. It's a wonderful way to play with a ball when you're feeling lazy—because you don't ever have to chase it.
It's also good to play this way when you're not feeling well and have to stay in bed.

Just think—there are so many people we talk about and yet these people never even lived, people like:

Jack Sprat
Peter Pan
Cinderella

Do you know any others?
Storybooks are so much fun—aren't they?

Climb the tree in your garden.
Isn't it great to be alone in the tree—high up in the sky?
You can hide in the leaves so no one will find you.
If you can find two strong branches to sit on, they can be like a chair and you can read a book.
If you want to make crazy sounds out loud, no one will stop you.
Or
If you just want to daydream—it's O.K.

Snuggle in your bed and
watch the round, yellow moon peeping through the window.
Isn't it interesting that the moon just stands and stares at you?
Do you wonder where the moon goes in the morning, when the night is over?

Play what children from generation to generation have played—finger plays. Children have always loved them and you will too!
The main thing to remember about finger plays is that there are no rules to follow.
If a finger wants to wiggle or slither—that's O.K.
If a finger wants to croak like a bullfrog or purr like a cat—that's O.K. too.

WIGGLE

I wiggle my fingers
I wiggle my toes

I wiggle my shoulders
I wiggle my nose
Now no more wiggles are left in me
So I will be still as still as can be.

Think about the wonders of paint.
Can paint glide?
Can it drag?
See the globs it makes.
Can it spread like magic on wet paper and in water too?
Paint can be made lighter or darker.
Colors can be mixed.
Did you ever make your paint swallow up all the colors to make "brown"?

Be a great magician.
All you need to do is put a piece of carbon paper between two sheets of drawing paper.
Then draw a picture on the top piece of paper.
NOW—ABRACADABRA! You have two pictures and you drew only one!
That's real magic!

If it can be arranged—
Try to take a tour through:
a dress factory
an automobile assembly line
a flour-milling plant
a lumberyard
a city-bus terminal
a meatpacking plant
Don't you find it very interesting?

Roll up an old bath towel
or
stuff an old pillowcase into the shape of a snake.
Tuck it on a windowsill and be proud of yourself for helping to keep drafts out and helping to save energy.

Look up at the top of a big tree.
What's going on up there?
Do you see birds
or
a raccoon?
Are there any nests?
Can you draw a picture of what you see?

Make telephones so you and your friend can talk to each other.
Here's all you have to do:
Get hold of two paper cups and a long string.
Glue the ends of the string to the bottom of the cups.
And then—talk.

Play "Follow the Leader."
Someone is chosen leader and everyone else has to follow.
If the leader raises arms, the others must follow.
If the leader hops on one foot, the others must follow.
If the leader goes up and down stairs, the others must do the same thing.
Even if the leader walks kind of silly, the others have to walk the same way.

Find out if you would be able to visit a food factory. There may be an ice cream factory you can visit.

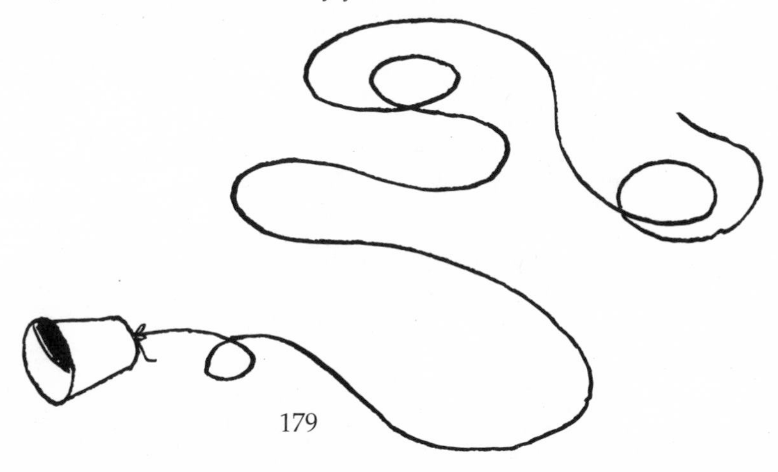

Wouldn't it be great to visit a pasta factory and watch the spaghetti popping out of the pipes and vats?

* Some factories have guided tours you can take. AND some of the tours have samples to taste!

Watch a big fat bumblebee buzzing at a rose.

Can you pretend you are a big fat bumblebee buzzing around the sweetness of a rose too?

Do some warm-up exercises with your parents.

Can you stretch way up high on your toes?

Can you touch your toes without bending your knees?

Can you jump and clap? Do pushups?

How about turning like a windmill?

Look down at the ground where you step.

How dark it must be underneath!

Do you wonder if the worms and the ants mind the darkness?

What are they doing down there? Are they creeping about the stones?

Do you think they hear you when you walk on the ground? Do they wonder what you're doing up there?

Take lessons on how to play a tonette

the recorder

the piano

or

any other instrument.

You'll have pleasure.

You'll give pleasure to others.

And

If the birds and animals hear you, they'll have pleasure too.

Go to the ice cream parlor with the money you earned for sweeping your neighbor's driveway—
and buy a double-scoop ice cream cone.

Look at the fallen flowers flying back to the branches of the trees.
Upps—Sorry! They're flitting butterflies!

Stuff a large, old tire with sand for a sandbox.
Of course—if it's for you—you'll keep the sand in the tire so it won't be scattered all over.
BUT
If it's for your little sister or brother, the sand will certainly get scattered.
You'll help them keep the sand inside and all clean—won't you?

Look for a daisy
and
when you find one recite:

"_______ loves you. _______ loves you not."
"_______ loves you. _______ loves you not,"

as you pluck off each petal.
When you plucked off the last petal, which one did you say?

Just suppose there were no written words.
Do you know that thousands of years ago, there weren't any written words? People just used pictures to "write."
Can you draw a picture to say fish?
rain?
a flower?
a boy or a girl?
Can you "write" a story with pictures?

Put out some nuts so a squirrel will come by.

Then, if you're lucky enough—watch where the squirrel goes with them.

(Be careful not to touch the fluffy squirrel. Squirrels can bite!)

When others are riding in their cars to the corner store and you're walking to the corner store—

Does it make you feel proud and good inside?

Find out about a lot of things by asking a lot of "whys."

Like:

Why do we see so many worms after a rain?

Why do bears sleep all winter?

Why do leaves fall from trees?

Are there other "whys" that come to you?

Go shopping to buy an anthill. Pet shops sell them and sometimes you can find them at a hobby shop or dime-store.

An anthill comes in a tight, flat container (so no one has to worry about the ants getting all over the house).

Watch what goes on inside that anthill and keep track of how the ant colony changes over several months.

WHAT FUN THEY ARE TO WATCH!

Is there a cocoon on a branch of a tree?

Does it look as if it's just about to split open?

Then—wait.

You'll soon have one of the wonderful surprises of your life.

Don't go away!

Go riding on your bike—or do you have a minibike?

Can you ride a bit with just one hand?

(But don't ride too fast or you'll land upside down!)

Think about feelings that everyone of us has:
how it felt when you got lost in a store
how it felt when you took your first plane ride
how it felt when your guppy died
how it felt when someone stole your wagon
How does it feel when you are about to get your story for the night—and then a kiss?

Make a touch bag.
Put all sorts of different things in a bag. Things like:
a small rock
a shell
or
some rough bark from a log, etc.
Then
Ask a friend to touch each thing with closed eyes and guess what is being touched.
How good are they at guessing?

Smear cold cream over a cookie sheet.
You can have a great time making swirling patterns or pretty pictures.
(Mud, of course, is good too for making swirling patterns and pictures—but cold cream is a lot easier to wash off—isn't it? Try it and see.)

Kiss your baby sister right in the middle of her belly button.

Make up a newspaper ad to sell
spaghetti
bananas
or
jelly beans.

Watch the gigantic cement mixer clattering and churning away mixing the cement, the sand, the rocks, and the water—
so that it's just right.
Then watch the concrete come down the shoot—
down to the space saved for the new sidewalk.
Doesn't the sidewalk look so nice when the workers smooth the concrete?
Did they press in the name of their company?

Make your own flying disk out of a round piece of cardboard or
by stapling two paper plates together.
And then toss it out into the air.
How far will it go?
Will your dog run after it and bring it back to you?

Don't peek.
Can you tell what was dropped?
Was it
a penny?
a key?
a shoe?
a book?
If a piece of paper were dropped, could you tell what it was?

Collect all the ribbon the family gets from presents. Notice how pretty it is—
different shiny colors
some wide, some skinny
some velvety
some with pretty flowers

Dip the ribbons lightly into globs of glue squeezed out in a jar lid and
make a beautiful piece of artwork with them.

Sit on the sidewalk and be a "sidewalk superintendent" as you watch the neighbor's dead tree being cut down.
BUT DON'T GET TOO CLOSE!

Besides enjoying animals as pets, think of other ways you're glad that there are animals.
Do they give us:
meat to eat?
skin to keep people warm?
wool for sweaters and blankets?
milk for grown-ups and children to drink?
help for carrying heavy loads?
Have you ever seen a "seeing eye" dog with a blind person?

If you had a whiff of these spices, could you tell what they were?
cinnamon bark?
oregano?
dried mint leaves?
a garlic clove?

Play "What Am I?"
Someone makes a sound and you try to guess what the sound is. You could have sounds like:
moo
clickety-clack
tick-tock
ding-dong-ding-dong
w-o-o-o-o-o
beep-beep
Be sure to take turns!

Go for a walk with an adult—but this time go for a walk you haven't walked before.

Is there a detour you can take?
What about walking down a back street?

Sack race with your friend. Get out two burlap sacks. Each of you stand in a sack, holding it up by each corner.
Who can hop or hobble faster?

Watch the rumbling train going by.
Do you like the clickety-click sound of the wheels?
Do you wonder if the train is carrying automobiles?
Can you count the freight cars?
Is the train carrying coal
food
or
people?
(Wouldn't you love to go on a train ride? Maybe you will someday.)

Look at the traffic lights blinking away. Do you know that traffic lights can talk too?
Green says "Go."
Red says "Stop."
and Yellow says "Watch out. I'm going to change to red!"
(BUT YOU MUST ALWAYS LOOK BEFORE YOU CROSS THE STREET!)

On your next shopping trip check:
Is the item made from recycled materials?
Is the packaging (the glass or plastic bottle or the box) recyclable?
Try to be a lover of the earth always.

Ask your family to find out where you can go maple-sugaring.
Maybe you'll get a chance to put the hot syrup on cold, cold snow.
(Oh—what good candy that makes!)

Most of us go to sleep at night. BUT the fireflies are busy lighting up.

So—some summer evening, keep your eyes open for some tiny lights flashing in your dark backyard.
Do you see some? Do you know what they are?
Yes! They're fireflies.
Try to catch one to put in a jar. Then put a lid with holes in it on your jar and see the firefly's glow lighting up your room.
(But—please do let it go free in the morning!)

Look up at the birds on top of your roof.
Don't they seem to be watching over the earth?

Look at the thick stem of your cactus plant.
Do you know what goes on inside?
This wonderful desert plant stores water in the stem
and
the prickles keep thirsty animals from eating it.
Clever—isn't it?
(Someday you may want to grow your own cactus garden.
But—be careful—DON'T TOUCH!)

Ask a grown-up to teach you how to tie a tie.
(You may have to wear one sooner than you think.)

If someone you know has a microscope, you must look at a butterfly's wings!

Play a game of "Toss and Catch" with a friend.
To play the game, each one makes a ball from aluminum foil
and then
you try to catch each ball in your cup as you toss them back and forth.

Do you have grapevines in your garden? How about making raisins from some of the grapes? (Any kind of grapes will do for it, but seedless grapes will make seedless raisins—and that would be better—wouldn't it?)

Here's what to do:

Pick the grapes.
Put them in a sunny window.
Spread them out so that the sun can get at all of them.
Cover the grapes with some cheesecloth to keep them clean.
Turn the grapes over from time to time.
and
Soon you will have raisins MADE BY YOU!

Draw a picture of you landing on top of a full moon
or
draw a picture of you on a giant rainbow.
(If you would like to have your dog with you on the moon or the rainbow, that would be good too.)

Squirm around on your stomach through tall grass near a small stream
and
find out what just went "CHIRP"!

Make believe your bed is a boat.
Then
all you have to do is
close your eyes
and
sail away!

Go outside with a big old paintbrush and a pail of water
and be a
SIDEWALK ARTIST.

Watch your mother nursing your baby brother or sister.
(Maybe Mother will let you burp the baby when the baby is done—wouldn't you love to do that?)

Nest your six Russian nesting dolls, those lovely little dolls that fit into one another and show us that life goes

on
and
on
and
on.

Snoop on the hummingbird.
Doesn't it look like a helicopter over a flower?

Make a totem pole by gluing empty spools of any size on top of one another.
If you like, you can draw or paint pictures on your totem pole, the way Native Americans did.

Look at the tulips that have opened up. They seem to look like little cups to let in the beautiful springtime—don't they?

If there is any chance at all—
If you want a real thrill—
Watch a baby chick come out of a little warm egg.

Find a pencil
crayon
or
chalk
and
scribble.

Go any way you want to.
(Don't tell anyone, but one of the greatest artists in the whole world—Leonardo da Vinci—was a scribbler too!)

Go to look at the nearby tree that was uprooted by the big storm and look carefully at the gigantic roots.

If you had three wishes, what would they be?
Can you draw them?

(You'll have to get up pretty early for this.)
Marvel at the lovely hibiscus flowers that open when the sun rises.
And then see how they close with the sunset.

Someday, watch your mother just to find out all the things she does to make a healthy, happy home for the family.
Can you name ten things she does?

Watch the rabbit scurrying about.
See its ears stand up straight and how big they are!
Do you think it would be easy for a rabbit to wear a hat?
Wouldn't it be wonderful if you could ever, ever get permission to take a rabbit to bed with you?

On a board, glue or nail bottle caps in the shape of your house number and place it in front of your house.
It makes your house look "special," doesn't it?

Get out the hula hoop and
spin it around
and
around
and
around.

 Play solitaire with a deck of cards.

Sometimes—
when you're told to "SIT UP NICELY!"
don't you feel as if you would like to do something besides eat your lunch?

Borrow the family's laundry basket.
Stand back and see how many times you can toss a ball into the basket.
How many times out of ten can you toss it in?

Choose up sides and play tag in your backyard until it's too dark to be able to see
or
until your mother calls you the third time to come in for supper!

Have a make-believe fight with a friend with crumpled newspaper balls.
But, when your father says, YOU MUST QUIT NOW—there's nothing to do but quit. Too bad—and you were having such fun!

See how good you are at balancing a marshmallow on your nose
and
can you walk with the marshmallow on your nose?

Just watch the sun
and
see how it slowly
dries up the soda pop
that the little girl spilled on the sidewalk.

Have you ever wondered what the gulls are doing as they fly back and forth in the sky?
Wouldn't you like to follow them?

See if your parents can spare some paper cups.
If you turn some of them upside down, you can make a "tent city."

Collect seeds.
Of course, it's easy to buy seeds, but did you know that you may have even more fun—
if you plant a seed you found yourself, especially if it's from a plant you love.
For example:
a helicopter seed from the neighbor's backyard
a pinecone you found on the way to your friend's house
(Pinecones have lots of seeds in them.)
the funny ball from the sycamore tree
a milkweed pod lying on the park grounds
Try a seed you found on the dandelion on your front lawn.

If there's an old unused alarm clock around
Find someone who loves to take things apart and put them together again.
You'll find it very interesting to see the inside of a clock and how the gears work.

Watch the house around the block being painted.
When one person is painting the house
doesn't it seem to take forever?
Or
When a whole bunch of people are painting it, doesn't it seem as if it took hardly any time at all?

* Would you like to be a housepainter someday and climb those tall ladders? It's scary—isn't it?

Roll up your body like a ball
and
tumble like a tumbleweed through the house.

See how wrong lots of people are about snakes.
Get out your pet snake. Look at it very close. See—it's not slimy. The snake is covered all over with dry scales!
Also, few snakes are dangerous. Your rock garden's garter snake isn't, but the rattlesnake IS!

Watch a dog chase a big fat cat
up the neighbor's weeping willow tree.

Just think of what it would be like if:
houses had no windows
birds didn't sing
every day were Sunday
we didn't have any friends
Wouldn't it be awful?

Look for a ladybug.
When you find a ladybug, ask her why she always likes to hug a daisy.

Have a javelin throw contest with your friends by seeing who can toss toothpicks the farthest.

Enjoy the shape, the feel, and color of some of the everyday things you have in your house, things like:
the vase in your living room
the pitcher on the dining room table
a cooking pot
even your ladle that scoops up soup.

Keep your eyes open while your parents drive
down the back roads
the dirt roads
the gravel roads
away from the main roads
so busy with traffic
and
stores
and
people.
(It's so different and such a treat—especially if you come across a farmer who has a little outdoor stand with freshly picked corn for you to take home.)

Listen to the beetles, bees, and the other bugs talk.
What do you think they talk about?
Do you think they talk about the weather?
or
what they ate for lunch?
or
the storm that's coming out their way?
Listen carefully!

Watch the excavator scooping out a gigantic load of earth.
Doesn't it almost look like a great big dinosaur stretching out its neck to scoop up a mound of earth and devour it?

Keep your eyes open for an old-fashioned wooden barrel.
If you're lucky enough to find one—
SHOUT A GREAT BIG
HE-LLLLLOOOOO into it.

* See if you can give yourself a free ride by rolling on it too.

Get out your collection of old unwanted keys.
Do you know that you can make sleigh bells by stringing keys onto a key ring?
(The bigger the keys, the louder the bells will sound. Try it. You'll see!)
How about sticking a key in your sister's pocket just to surprise her?

Make up a library in your own home or backyard.
Collect books
comic books
magazines
records
and lend them out to your neighbor friends.
Can you arrange to have a "story hour" time too? Any grown-up would be glad to help.

Go into the kitchen and make yourself a peanut butter and jelly sandwich.
If there's a banana around—put that on the top.
YUMMY!

Play a game of checkers or dominoes with your dad.

See if a grown-up will go to the park with you to rent a row-boat and go rowing with you on the quiet lake.
Can you see any fish?

What animals are on the lily pads?
Do you see any insects gliding on the top of the water?
Are there any pebbles you'd like to carry home in the bag you brought?

Listen to the sounds in your house just before you go to bed.
Do you hear:
an airplane flying overhead?
someone flushing the toilet or taking a shower?
the neighbor's dog barking to come inside?
a garage door slamming?
Is your sister practicing her piano?
Is your brother using the typewriter for a homework assignment?
IS THAT FAUCET DRIPPING AGAIN?

When you put on your clothes or help put on the baby's clothes, sing to the tune of "Jingle Bells":
"Here's your shirt,
Here's your shirt,
Here's your bright red shirt," etc.

*You can do this any time during the day, and maybe soon you'll hear the baby trying to sing along with you.

When you look at that white birch tree on your neighbor's lawn—
Doesn't it look as if it's wrapped in paper?
or
like it's wearing a nightie?
(Please don't take the bark off. That would kill the lovely birch tree.)

Think about your home.
Isn't it more than rooms with a roof over them?
Isn't your home a place where there's someone to love

and
a place where there's someone to love you?
Isn't it the dearest spot on earth?

Pretend you are a big clock and make the sound T-I-C-K T-O-C-K,
T-I-C-K T-O-C-K.
Pretend you are a small clock and make the sound tick, tock,
tick, tock.
Pretend you are a very tiny clock and make the sound like
tick, tock,
tick, tock,
tick, tock,
tick, tock.

* Move your arms around as you say your tick-tocks.

Play around with straws and see what you can do with them.
You can make a straw sculpture by squeezing the end of one straw into the end of another straw. If the whole straw is too big to use, just make it smaller.
Then:
Bend and curve the straws.
Squeeze them.
And make anything you want from them.

When the sun is strong and the day is s-o-o-o-o hot—
Find a shady spot
and
sit
and
sit
and
sit.

Walk down the block just to see what all the different things the outside of the houses are made of.

Do you see any made of wood?
  of bricks?
  of stucco?
  of stone?
Are there any that are made of wood *and* brick?
  stucco *and* wood?
    or
  any other combination?

Try to figure this out:
Do you know what goes in when the sun shines?
And this thing comes out when it rains.
If it's a nice, clear day and you look for it
You'll be looking in vain.
(Yup—it's an earthworm!)
  Can you make up more riddles for guessing?

Listen to the music on the radio.
Do you think of birds?
  flowers?
  your friends?
  going to the country?
  a basketful of brownies?
    Or
Do you just feel like sitting and feeling good inside?

Watch the fly that dove right into your bowl of soup!
Do you think that flies like soup too?

Look in the basement.
Is there a box of nails and screws all mixed up?
Help sort them out and put them in empty baby-food jars or boxes.
How much easier it will be for your parents to find what they need!

Think hard.
How many things can you name that are "wettish"?

Is a watermelon "wettish"?
Is a slice of bread "wettish"?

Have someone help you address a letter to your own house.
Then find out what happens when you mail it.
Did it come back to you the next day?
Isn't it fun getting mail?

Play baseball with your friend.
If you don't have a real bat, you'll see that you can have just as much fun if you use a stick or a sturdy piece of a branch for a bat.

Sit in the backyard under the apple tree
and
help string the green beans for canning.

If you can visit a farm—
Watch a little pig cool off in a nice mud puddle.
If there's another little pig cooling off—watch them play.
Don't they play like little puppy dogs?

Think about this:
Birds are animals.
So are fish.
So are worms.
Frogs and turtles are animals.
And what are we?

Try this—
Keep your legs straight
and
see if you can bend down and touch your toes.
(How many times can you do it—IF you can?)

Think of how nice it would be if your mother could rock you to sleep the way she used to.
Can you remember the lullabies she sang?
Why not sing them together?

Type a letter to a friend on an old manual typewriter.
(Typing with one finger is just fine and so is any spelling you use.)

Look at the pretty evergreen trees.
How birds love the evergreen trees.
Evergreen trees shelter them from rain and cold.
Wouldn't you like an evergreen too if you were a bird?

You're having a hard time learning to tie your shoes?
Don't give up.
Just think of this wonderful old, old story:

Two frogs were hopping along and they accidentally dropped into a bucket of milk. One of them said, "There's no sense trying to get out of here," so he dropped to the bottom of the bucket and drowned.
The other frog said, "I'm going to keep trying till I get out of here." And he kept thrashing his legs till the milk turned into butter—AND HE HOPPED OUT!

(Now get busy and learn to tie your shoes. Don't give up!)

On a cold winter day—
Blow out slowly.
Watch your steamy breath.
Doesn't it look like smoke?

Smell a rose.

Listen to people talk.
Did you ever hear them use any of these "comparison" words? Aren't they fun to hear? And isn't it easier to know just what a person means when such words are used?
Here are some you might hear:

as green as grass
as sweet as honey
as quick as a wink
as sly as a fox
as warm as toast
as clear as mud
as slow as molasses

Can you make some up yourself?

Dig up a shovelful of dirt.
Spread it all out on newspaper
and
see how many animals are living in it.
Do you see any
centipedes?
millipedes?
a beetle or two?
or
some other wonderful creatures?

Pretend you are Jack Frost.
Have you ever seen Jack Frost?
You haven't?
Well—nobody in the world has ever seen Jack Frost.
But—we all know he's around when he:
pinches and bites our toes
and
makes our fingers numb.
DON'T WE?
Think of all the things Jack Frost can do.
He can give a tree a new autumn suit.
He can make walnuts come tumbling down.
Pumpkins are ripened by Jack Frost.
Jack Frost can make you cover up for sleep too—can't he?

Ask a grown-up to set up three objects, one of which is different from the other two. Something like this:
two dress shoes and one sneaker
two books for reading and one book to color
Do you know which one doesn't belong?

Watch how a grown-up plugs a plug into a socket.
Watch a grown-up jack up a car.
Isn't it fun to see how a tire is changed?
See how storm windows are taken down and how screens are put up.
You won't be able to do these things all by yourself yet.
But someday you will. And then someday someone will watch you.
Isn't it a great way to learn things?

Make a book about YOU with cut-out pictures from magazines and newspapers. Or you can draw the pictures.
The pictures could be of:
babies and the things that babies do
children playing with toys you like to play with

foods you like to eat
pictures of the kind of work your parents do
pictures of a house that looks something like yours
pictures of animal pets like yours, etc.

If you can give up the doughnut you got for lunch—
Spread peanut butter on it.
Stick birdseed on it.
Hang the doughnut from a string onto a branch
of a tree
AND SEE IF BIRDS LIKE DOUGHNUTS TOO!

Try to make as many letters of the alphabet with your fingers as you can.
An "I" is easy and so is an "O." Try those first and then see how many others you can make.

Get out the small (but sturdy) trash container.
Tip it on its side
and
you can be a cowboy or cowgirl riding a horse!

When it's hot inside
open up your window
and
listen to the lovely sounds of your wind chimes outdoors.
(Aren't they especially pretty to hear when there's a little breeze?)

Spend some time with a flower.
Touch the petals.
Get very close to smell the flower. Did the pollen get on your nose?
How many colors are on that one flower?
Do you see any patterns?
WHAT A WORK OF ART IS A FLOWER!

Find a nice chunk of wood and make believe it's a taxicab.
Pick up passengers as you drive it along—
and
don't forget to charge for the ride!
(Or—do you want your rides to be free?)

Jump rope with your friends.
Just as dandelions make their first appearance in the spring—so do children get out their ropes and jump rope.
Here are some catchy jingles children have enjoyed jumping to for many, many years:

Charlie over the water,
Charlie over the sea.
Charlie caught a blackbird
But he can't catch me.

Hippity hop to the barbershop
Hippity hop to the barbershop
To buy a stick of candy.
One for you and one for me
And one for sister Mandy.

Feel a rock.
Did you ever wonder what a rock went through to feel that way?
Did the rain fall on it?
Did the winter ice crack it?
Would you want to guess how old the rock might be?

See how good you are at telling a hard-boiled egg from a raw egg. Can you tell by looking?
If you really want to find out—just spin each egg (be careful not to crack it), and you will find out that the hard-boiled egg spins faster and longer than the raw egg. Try it.

Go square dancing at the nearby community center.
If you don't know how to square dance yet, just go down to watch.
"Right hand! Left hand! Around you go!
Now go back-to-back in a do-si-do!
Swing your arms and shout 'Yah-hoo!'"

Save corks of any size you can get hold of because they make great people or animals:
Just add a few toothpicks
some paper and glue
and
use felt-tip markers to make noses and eyes and other important things.

If you have a space where you can't hurt yourself—
Try walking backward—
tiny steps
sliding steps
and
big giant steps.
Careful!

Watch how your goldfish wiggle
swiggle
scurry
whiz
and
leap about all day long
without a sound.
Wouldn't you love to have your goldfish come out and play with you if they only could?

Pretend you are a tough giant—
A—R U M P F!
Show how giants eat.

How do giants take a bath?
Where do giants sleep?
Do giants have babies? And how do they take care of their babies?
Do giants have friends the way you do?
What kind of steps do giants take?
G I A N T   S T E P S?
Can you take G I A N T   S T E P S?

Hurry! Look!
There's a sleeping bird perched on a tree.
It's going to fall off!
(No it won't. Do you know why? Its toes hook onto a branch very tight, the way you would hold a stick or a baseball bat with both hands.)

Go out and watch the ice cream man coming down the street in his little ice cream truck.
See how he fills the cones with mounds of vanilla, chocolate, and cherry ice cream.
Doesn't it make your mouth water?
Also
Did you ever wonder where the ice cream man puts all the ice cream at night?

When you see swans gliding along with their arched necks and lovely feathers—
Don't they look as though they own the pond?

Visit a rock quarry with the family and go fossil hunting
or
try hunting for fossils in the rock layers of a road cut.
See if you can find a trilobite. If you don't know about trilobites, look them up in a fossil book. You'll find out about other fossils too.
(Someday you may want to start a fossil collection. Someday you may even want to be a geologist!)

Think about how wonderful it would be if
you could get
smaller
and
smaller
and
walk up and down a buttercup.

Get out your old pants and dig into your pockets.
WOW—what treasures!
a dead beetle
your old skate key
a penny
a white stone
and
raisins too dried up to eat.

Look at the mushrooms that popped up overnight.
Aren't their tops graceful and ripply?
And the shapes—aren't they so strange and sort of weird?
Some look like tiny umbrellas—don't they?
Do you like the colors they have?
(Pretty as mushrooms are—you won't eat them though—will you? Because some mushrooms are poisonous to eat. Eat only the ones that are sold at food markets.)

Go with someone to the gas station.
Can you help turn the lever so it switches the pump on?
Can you help put the hose nozzle into the tank?
Notice how it shuts off when the tank is filled to the top.
See how it shuts off all by itself.
Wouldn't you like to be able to fill the tank all by yourself someday?

Visit your old neighbor friend down the block.
Watch him sitting on his porch whittling with his knife.
Doesn't he seem to love what he's doing?
Do you think he would let you have the curled cedar shavings to play with?

On a great big sheet of paper along a wall
put out some crayons or paint and brushes
and
everyone pitch in to make a mural.
How about a mural of:
Our Family?
The Work People Do?
People of Different Lands?
Our Garden?
What else?

Join a nearby community center. Most have great childrens' programs, like:
swimming classes
sewing classes
all kinds of crafts
and they usually have summer camp programs for children.

* It's also a great place to meet other children.

Learn your telephone number by heart.
Then learn to dial the emergency number.
Then learn the numbers of your relatives
your friends
your doctor
any other number good to know.

* It might be a good idea to practice on a toy telephone first if you have one. When you can use a telephone all by yourself it will really make you "feel big"!

Try your hand at juggling.
Try juggling a stone
a nectarine
or
a bagel.
(But don't let the bagel drop to the floor. You wouldn't want to eat a dirty bagel, would you?)

Go down the block to visit the new kid who moved in last week
and
hang around with him for a while.
(Just be sure you get home in time for dinner!)

Play kickball with your friend in your driveway.
Here's how you play.
One of your friends rolls the ball to you and you kick it.
Then you roll the ball and your friend kicks it.
Simple—isn't it?
and
lots of fun too!

Go for a walk—just to collect dried-up flowers.
That sounds like a strange thing to do—doesn't it?
But—
Did you know that flowers make seeds?
Put the seeds you find in a container and put it in the refrigerator so that they can "feel" the winter.
In the spring, you can plant your seeds in the garden.
You'll be very surprised at what comes up!

If the nearby school
community center
or
museum's science group

is going out to plant trees—
find out if you can go along with them. You'd like to help save the Earth too—wouldn't you?

When you go walking in the park—
Keep your eyes open mostly to see if there are any statues in it.
Some parks have lots of statues
and
some parks have only one.
(Someday maybe you'll find a beautiful, beautiful statue of David that was done by a famous Italian, Michelangelo, hundreds of years ago. You'll love it!)

Play a "touching" game with your friend.
Close your eyes and guess what you're touching.
Try these:
a carrot
a potato
a cucumber
a grape
spinach
Can you tell a grapefruit from an orange?

Soak berries
roots
twigs
vegetables
and
bark
in water and see if the color of the water changes.
Now you can see how people long ago dyed their cloth pretty colors.

Help load the family car with lots of food
and
drive
miles

and
miles
to visit a relative you haven't seen for a long, long time.

Go downtown someday and look at the great big buildings.
Look carefully.
Do you see any buildings made of
red sandstone?
granite?
Are you lucky enough to find one made of marble?
(Look closely—does the marble look as if it has beautiful rivers flowing through it?)

On a cold, blustery day when everything is so dark and gray—
Go visit a greenhouse.
You'll feel so much better when you see the lovely flowers
that are grown indoors
and
see the workers—how they've made pretty bouquets and corsages
AND
OH—HOW EVERYTHING SMELLS SO NICE!

Go shopping with Mother at the health food store.
Have you ever tried mung bean sprouts to put in your salad?
dipped honey on papaya?
sprinkled wheat germ on your brown rice?
added sunflower seeds to your homemade oatmeal cookies?
cut up pieces of tofu for your stir-fry?
Can you think of many things more delicious than topping whole wheat bread with freshly made peanut butter?

Get out your butterfly net and try to catch a butterfly.
If you do catch a butterfly, keep it in a wide-mouthed jar with a piece of screen or netting over the top so the butterfly will have air to breathe.

Enjoy the butterfly for a while.
Then—
Give it its freedom.
(There's really no good reason to let the poor little butterfly die in a jar—is there? Wouldn't you feel happier if you knew the little butterfly could fly around and make other people happy too?)

Have a "Round Robin" story.
A "Round Robin" story goes like this:
One person makes up the beginning of a story, tells a little of the story—then stops at a very important part.
Then the next person starts the story where the person stopped.
And then the next person has a turn.
And then the next person—
Till everyone has a turn and the last person ends the story.

* Try a "Round Robin" story and see how much fun it is!

Be a very special kind of artist who can make beautiful things with very special materials. For example:

Make a picture from torn-out pieces of newspapers.
Can you make a tree? a dog? a person?

Make a picture from cut-out shapes of circles, squares, triangles, and rectangles.
Can you make a ball? a tent? a table? What else?

Watch the guppies in your fish tank being born.

See how they come out live from the mother and can go swimming "on their own" right away. (They don't have to take swimming lessons the way you do!)

If you have a tank of tropical fish—the babies are born from a cluster of eggs.

Even if you don't have a fish tank but can get near a stream or a pond, you can bring home a fish in a pail of water,
watch it for a while
and
then take the fish back to its home again.
(Wouldn't you love to try that sometime?)

Get hold of a bunch of toothpicks and have someone show you how to write numbers in roman numerals with them.

For example, it's easy to make the number "1," "2," all the way to 12.

And it's "pie" to go all the way up to 20.
Try it!

Get out your dad's binoculars and—

Watch a bird fly high into the sky.
Watch a flock of migrating birds.
Look for a mother sparrow teaching her young to fly.
Can you find a robin scratching for worms in the damp earth?
Can you see a chickadee singing his cheery song high in a tree?
Look very carefully—you might be able to come up close to an oriole's nest, which looks like a pocket dangling from a limb.

(That's especially great for oriole babies, which can get a free ride when the breezes blow.)

Help a grown-up nail a box on the outside windowsill where you eat.

If you do, you'll have bird visitors you can watch every day of the year.

A good idea is to feed the birds "cafeteria style" so that the different birds can choose from the different foods.

Just about all kitchen scraps could be used:

apple cores
stale bread
fresh or cooked vegetables
all kinds of soup

See if the birds like PIZZA.

Sometime—get up very early in the morning and watch the sun rise.

Someday—
Go shuffling through crackling leaves (oh—so idly)
and
just be alone
to see
to feel
to think
to dream.